JOHN STOTT BIBLE STUDIES

20 Studies with Commentary for Individuals or Groups

Romans

Encountering the Gospel's Power

John
STOTT

Inter-Varsity Press
Nottingham, England

IVP Connect
An imprint of InterVarsity Press
Downers Grove, Illinois

InterVarsity Press, USA
P.O. Box 1400, Downers Grove, IL 60515-1426, USA
World Wide Web: www.ivpress.com
Email: email@ivpress.com

Inter-Varsity Press, England
Norton Street, Nottingham NG7 3HR, England
Website: www.ivpbooks.com
Email: ivp@ivpbooks.com

InterVarsity Press®, USA, is the book-publishing division of InterVarsity Christian Fellowship/USA®,
a student movement active on campus at hundreds of universities, colleges and schools of nursing in
the United States of America, and a member movement of the International Fellowship of Evangelical
Students. For information about local and regional activities, write Public Relations Dept., InterVarsity
Christian Fellowship/USA, 6400 Schroeder Rd., P.O. Box 7895, Madison, WI 53707-7895, or visit the IVCF
website at <www.intervarsity.org>.

Inter-Varsity Press, England, is closely linked with the Universities and Colleges Christian Fellowship, a
student movement connecting Christian Unions in universities and colleges throughout Great Britain, and
a member movement of the International Fellowship of Evangelical Students. Website: www.uccf.org.uk.

This study guide is based on and includes excerpts adapted from Romans ©1994 by John R. W. Stott.

Design: Cindy Kiple
Images: Arpad Benedek/iStockphoto

USA ISBN 978-0-8308-2165-5
UK ISBN 978-1-84474-317-9

Printed in the United States of America ∞

P   23 22 21 20 19 18 17 16 15 14 13 12 11 10 9 8 7 6 5 4 3 2 1

Y   27 26 25 24 23 22 21 20 19 18 17 16 15 14 13 12 11 10 09 08

Introducing Romans

Romans is a kind of Christian manifesto of freedom through Jesus Christ. Freedom from the holy wrath of God upon all ungodliness. Freedom from alienation into reconciliation. Freedom from the condemnation of God's law. Freedom from the fear of death. Freedom from ethnic conflict. Freedom to give ourselves to the loving service of God and others.

Paul was probably writing the Romans from Corinth during the three months he spent "in Greece" (Acts 20:2) just before sailing east. Paul was evidently apprehensive about his forthcoming visit to Jerusalem where he was taking money which the Greek churches had contributed for the poverty-stricken Christians in Judea. For Paul this was a symbol of Jewish-Gentile solidarity in the body of Christ. He was urging the Roman Christians to join him in praying for his personal safety and that the Jewish Christians would accept his gift. Paul was also writing to let the Romans know that he was planning a visit to them after visiting Jerusalem.

Getting to Know the Romans
A church had already come into being in Rome, perhaps through Jewish Christians who had returned home from Jerusalem after Pentecost (Acts 2:10). It was a mixed community consisting of both Jews and Gentiles, with Gentiles in the majority, and there was considerable conflict between these groups. This conflict was primarily not over ethnic issues, but theology. The

Jewish Christians were proud of their favored status before God, and the Gentile Christians of their freedom from the law.

A Message for Us
In his ministry of reconciliation between the Jews and the Gentiles, Paul develops two themes and interweaves them beautifully. The first is the justification of guilty sinners by God's grace alone in Christ, irrespective of status or works. This is the most humbling and equaling of all Christian truths. The second is that the people of God are no longer defined by descent, circumcision or culture, but according to faith in Jesus. So "there is no difference" now between Jews and Gentiles (Romans 3:22).

The call to unity is just as relevant to us today as we continue to face tensions in the body of Christ over ethnicity and theology. May we hear and respond to God's call to us in Romans.

Suggestions for Individual Study
1. As you begin each study, pray that God will speak to you through his Word.

2. Read the introduction to the study and respond to the question that follows it. This is designed to help you get into the theme of the study.

3. The studies are written in an inductive format designed to help you discover for yourself what Scripture is saying. Each study deals with a particular passage so that you can really delve into the author's meaning in that context. Read and reread the passage to be studied. The questions are written using the language of the New International Version, so you may wish to use that version of the Bible. The New Revised Standard Version is also recommended.

4. Each study includes three types of questions. *Observation* questions ask about the basic facts: who, what, when, where and how. *Interpretation* questions delve into the meaning of the passage. *Application* questions (also found in the "Apply" section) help you discover the implications of the text for growing in Christ. These three keys unlock the treasures of Scripture.

Write your answers to the study questions in the spaces provided or in a personal journal. Writing can bring clarity and deeper understanding of yourself and of God's Word.

5. In the studies you will find some commentary notes designed to give help with complex verses by giving further biblical and cultural background and contextual information. The notes in the studies are not designed to answer the questions for you. They are to help you along as you learn to study the Bible for yourself. After you have worked through the questions and notes in the guide, you may want to read the accompanying commentary by John Stott in the Bible Speaks Today series. This will give you more information about the text.

6. Move to the "Apply" section. These questions will help you connect the key biblical themes to your own life. Putting the application into practice is one of the keys to growing in Christ.

7. Use the guidelines in the "Pray" section to focus on God, thanking him for what you have learned and praying about the applications that have come to mind.

Suggestions for Members of a Group Study

1. Come to the study prepared. Follow the suggestions for individual study mentioned above. You will find that careful preparation will greatly enrich your time spent in group discussion.

2. Be willing to participate in the discussion. The leader of your group will not be lecturing. Instead, she or he will be encouraging the members of the group to discuss what they have learned. The leader will be asking the questions that are found in this guide.

3. Stick to the topic being discussed. Your answers should be based on the verses which are the focus of the discussion and not on outside authorities such as commentaries or speakers. These studies focus on a particular passage of Scripture. Only rarely should you refer to other portions of the Bible. This allows for everyone to participate on equal ground and for in-depth study.

4. Be sensitive to the other members of the group. Listen attentively

when they describe what they have learned. You may be surprised by their insights! Each question assumes a variety of answers. Many questions do not have "right" answers, particularly questions that aim at meaning or application. Instead the questions push us to explore the passage more thoroughly.

When possible, link what you say to the comments of others. Also, be affirming whenever you can. This will encourage some of the more hesitant members of the group to participate.

5. Be careful not to dominate the discussion. We are sometimes so eager to express our thoughts that we leave too little opportunity for others to respond. By all means participate! But allow others to also.

6. Expect God to teach you through the passage being discussed and through the other members of the group. Pray that you will have an enjoyable and profitable time together, but also that as a result of the study you will find ways that you can take action individually and/or as a group.

7. It will be helpful for groups to follow a few basic guidelines. These guidelines, which you may wish to adapt to your situation, should be read at the beginning of the first session.

☐ Anything said in the group is considered confidential and will not be discussed outside the group unless specific permission is given to do so.

☐ We will provide time for each person present to talk if he or she feels comfortable doing so.

☐ We will talk about ourselves and our own situations, avoiding conversation about other people.

☐ We will listen attentively to each other.

☐ We will be very cautious about giving advice.

8. If you are the group leader, you will find additional suggestions at the back of the guide.

1
GOSPEL POWER

Romans 1:1-17

W hat would it be like to live as a Christian in first-century Rome? You would be in the capital city of the world empire. The greatest sports, art and politics are centered in your city. You can hear a dozen languages in your streets, and religions of all sorts blend in the stew. You have heard of Christianity from a Jew who was present at an incredible event some thirteen hundred miles away in Jerusalem when a room shook, fire appeared, people spoke in tongues, and everyone talked about a martyr named Jesus who had died as a criminal then came back to life. This Jewish convert who had become a Christian didn't last long in Jerusalem, though. Not looking forward to martyrdom himself, he shipped off to the relative safety of Rome—and told his story: the story of Jesus. You believed. But what had you committed to? What is this new faith? A letter from the apostle Paul offers some answers.

Open

■ When and how did you first come in contact with the power of the gospel?

Study

■ *Read Romans 1:1-7.* Letter-writing conventions vary from culture to culture. We address our correspondent first ("Dear Joan") and identify ourselves only at the end ("Yours sincerely, John"). In the ancient world, however, the custom was to reverse the order, the writer announcing himself or herself first and the correspondent next ("John to Joan, greetings!"). Paul normally followed the convention of his day, but here he deviates from it by giving a much more elaborate description of himself than usual, in relation to the gospel.

1. What information about the gospel do you find in these verses?

2. Paul says in verse 6 that through the gospel we are "called to belong." How have you experienced that sense of belonging?

3. In verse 5 Paul speaks of "obedience that comes from faith." How are obedience and faith naturally connected?

4. Review verses 1-7. What do you learn about Paul?

about the Romans?

Summary: "God is the most important word in this epistle," Leon Morris has written. "Romans is a book about God. No topic is treated with anything like the frequency of God. Everything Paul touches in this letter he relates to God. . . . There is nothing like it elsewhere." (*The Epistle to the Romans* [InterVarsity Press, 1988], p. 40.) So the Christian good news is *the gospel of God.* The apostles did not invent it; it was revealed and entrusted to them by God.

---

5. *Read Romans 1:8-17.* In what different ways does Paul express his affection for the Romans (vv. 8-15)?

---

6. What do these verses reveal about Paul's relationship with God?

---

7. Paul knows about the reciprocal blessings of Christian fellowship, and although he is an apostle, he is not too proud to acknowledge his need for it. In verse 12 Paul says that he hopes that he and the Romans will be "mutually encouraged by each other's faith." Why is mutual encouragement valuable to Christians?

---

8. Focus on Paul's declaration in verses 16-17. What do these verses reveal about the power of the gospel?

---

9. This passage uses important words like *gospel, salvation, righteousness* and *faith.* How are these terms related to each other?

10. This section of Paul's letter ends with the famous phrase "The righteous will live by faith." In practical terms, what does this mean?

Summary: I once heard James Stewart of Edinburgh, in a sermon on this text, make the perceptive comment that "there's no sense in declaring that you're not ashamed of something unless you've been tempted to feel ashamed of it." And without doubt Paul knew this temptation. . . . How then did Paul (and how shall we) overcome the temptation to be ashamed of the gospel? He tells us. It is by remembering that the very same message, which some people despise for its weakness, is in fact *the power of God for the salvation of everyone who believes.* How do we know this? In the long run, only because we have experienced its saving power in our own lives. Has God reconciled us to himself through Christ, forgiven our sins, made us his children, put his Spirit within us, begun to transform us, and introduced us into his new community? Then how can we possibly be ashamed of the gospel?

Apply

■ What power have you seen the gospel exercise in your life? What power would you like it to have?

Paul says in verses 15-16, "I am so eager to preach. . . . I am not ashamed of the gospel." What can you do that expresses a similar enthusiasm for Christ?

Pray

■ In verse 8 Paul says, "I thank my God through Jesus Christ for all of you." Who can you thank God for and why? Take time right now to do that.

2
A DOWNWARD SPIRAL

Romans 1:18-32

*T*he very mention of God's wrath is calculated nowadays to cause people embarrassment and even amazement. How can anger be attributed to the all-holy God? Yet in this section of Romans we see the connection between the previous topic of the gospel of God and the wrath of God. Let me try to clarify the stages of the argument by engaging Paul in dialogue.

Paul: *I am not ashamed of the gospel* (v. 16).

Q: Why not, Paul?

Paul: *Because it is the power of God for the salvation of everyone who believes* (v. 16).

Q: How so, Paul?

Paul: Because *in the gospel a righteousness from God is revealed,* that is, God's way of justifying sinners (v. 17).

Q: But why is this necessary, Paul?

Paul: Because *the wrath of God is being revealed from heaven against all the godlessness and wickedness of men who suppress the truth by their wickedness* (v. 18).

Q: But how have people suppressed the truth, Paul?

Paul: Because *what may be known about God is plain to them. . . .*
For since the creation of the world God's invisible qualities . . . have been
clearly seen (vv. 19-20).

Open
■ What comes to your mind when you think of "the wrath of God"?

Study
■ *Read Romans 1:18-23.* Human anger, although there is such a thing as
righteous indignation, is mostly very unrighteous. It is an irrational and
uncontrollable emotion, containing much vanity, animosity, malice and the
desire for revenge. It should go without saying that God's anger is absolutely
free of all such poisonous ingredients. The wrath of God is almost totally
different from human anger. It does not mean that God loses his temper,
flies into a rage, or is ever malicious, spiteful or vindictive. The alternative
to wrath is not love but neutrality in the moral conflict. And God is not
neutral. On the contrary, his wrath is his holy hostility to evil, his refusal to
condone it or come to terms with it, his just judgment upon it.

1. Verse 18 begins "The wrath of God is being revealed." Why, according
to verses 18-23?

2. Verse 20 says that these people are "without excuse." Why, according
to verses 18-20?

3. Mentally review some of your own experiences with God's creation.

What do these reveal to you about God?

---

4. Verse 21 says that the people described here "knew God." What is dangerous about knowing about God but not acting on that knowledge (vv. 21-23)?

---

5. What do you think would happen to a person whose heart is "darkened" as verse 21 describes?

Summary: There are degrees to the knowledge of God, and these phrases cannot possibly refer to the full knowledge of him enjoyed by those who have been reconciled to him through Christ. For what Paul says here is that through general revelation people can know God's power, deity and glory (not his saving grace through Christ), and that this knowledge is enough not to save them but rather to condemn them, because they do not live up to it. Instead, they *suppress the truth by their wickedness* (v. 18), so that they *are without excuse* (v. 20). It is against this wilful human rebellion that God's wrath is revealed.

---

6. *Read Romans 1:24-32.* Three times in this passage Paul repeats the phrase "God gave them over." What did God give them over to?

7. What is your mental picture of each of these three downward spirals?

8. Verses 29-30 include sins like envy and murder, arrogance and God-hating, faithlessness and ruthlessness. What does the variety in this list suggest about the nature of sin?

9. What makes you uneasy about verses 18-32?

When we hear of God's wrath, we usually think of "thunderbolts from heaven, and earthly cataclysms and flaming majesty," yet here we learn that his anger goes "quietly and invisibly" to work in handing sinners over to themselves (Stephen C. Neill, *The Wrath and Peace of God* [CLS, 1943]), p. 12f.). God abandons stubborn sinners to their willful self-centeredness, and the resulting process of moral and spiritual degeneration is to be understood as a judicial act of God. This is the revelation of God's wrath from heaven (v. 18).

10. In verses 24, 26 and 28 God gave the people what they wanted. Why are these kinds of temptations dangerous?

11. Verse 32 says that these people deserve spiritual death. Why?

Summary: We have come to the end of Paul's portrayal of depraved Gentile society. Its essence lies in the antithesis between what people know and what they do. God's wrath is specifically directed against those who deliberately suppress truth for the sake of evil. "Dark as the picture here is drawn," wrote Charles Hodge, "it is not so dark as that presented by the most distinguished Greek and Latin authors, of their own countrymen" (*A Commentary on Romans* [1835; Banner of Truth Trust, 1972], p. 43). Paul was not exaggerating.

Apply

■ What sins in this downward spiral do you personally need to work on resisting?

What do you know about God that would help keep you out of this downward spiral?

Pray

■ Paul wrote in 1 Corinthians 10:13, "No temptation has seized you except what is common to man. And God is faithful; he will not let you be tempted beyond what you can bear. But when you are tempted, he will also provide a way out so that you can stand up under it." Talk to God about what tempts you to sin—and your own lapses toward the downward spiral of Romans 1. Ask God's forgiveness. Invite his strength to help you overcome future temptation in the same area "so that you can stand up under it."

3
GOD'S FAIRNESS

Romans 2:1-16

*J*udgment is a nasty word to many of us. We visualize a tired judge in traffic court who in the few seconds allotted to our case shows no sympathy for our five (or twenty-five) miles over the limit. Or our minds flash to an ugly scene with a parent where we were judged with unrelenting harshness with the result that we still sense a nagging guilt—as if we must have done something wrong, even if we can't quite think what it was. Sometimes we picture God, in spite of the "tender shepherd images," as an all-seeing eye who knows far more about us than we wish. And we long to crawl somewhere deep inside ourselves and hide. But if we must have a judge, we would surely want him to be fair.

Open

■ If you could live your life without personal guilt or judgment, would you choose that? Explain.

Study

1. *Read Romans 2:1-11.* The underlying theme of this section is the judgment of God upon self-appointed judges. The verses can be divided into two sections: 1-4 and 5-11. What qualities of God's judgment does

each section illustrate?

2. According to verses 1-4, why is it dangerous to judge someone else?

3. What is the difference between human judgment and God's judgment (vv. 1-4)?

4. Look more carefully at verse 4. How might God's judgment be a kindness?

5. Focus on verses 5-11. What does this passage reveal about the "day of God's wrath"?

6. Verse 11 says, "God does not show favoritism." In view of the preceding verses in that paragraph, what does this statement mean?

7. What impact does God's refusal to show favoritism have on you personally? (Consider your current relationship with God as well as your relationships with other people.)

Summary: Paul uncovers in these verses a strange human foible, namely our tendency to be critical of everybody except ourselves. We even gain a vicarious satisfaction from condemning in others the very faults we excuse in ourselves. Freud called this moral gymnastic "projection," but Paul described it centuries before Freud. This device enables us simultaneously to retain our sins and our self-respect. It is a convenient arrangement, but also both slick and sick.

---

8. *Read Romans 2:12-16.* What, according to these verses, is the relationship between God's law and his judgment?

---

9. What example do you see of God's fairness when he judges Gentiles—who did not have his law as a part of their history?

God will be absolutely even-handed in judgment. The way people have sinned (in knowledge or ignorance of the law) will be the way they will be judged, considering whether they have lived up to their knowledge. This is a theoretical or hypothetical statement, of course, since no human being has ever fully obeyed the law (Romans 3:20). So there is no possibility of salvation by that road. But Paul is writing about judgment, not about salvation.

---

10. Verse 15 speaks of the conscience. Why is a conscience important in this setting?

11. What can we do to cultivate a healthy conscience?

Summary: Until the law has done its work of exposing and condemning our sin, we are not ready to hear the gospel of justification. True, it is often said that we should address ourselves to people's conscious needs and not try to induce in them feelings of guilt that they do not have. This is a misconception, however. Human beings are moral beings by creation. That is to say, not only do we experience an inner urge to do what we believe to be right, but we also have a sense of guilt and remorse when we have done what we know to be wrong. There is of course such a thing as false guilt. But guilt feelings which are aroused by wrongdoing are healthy. They rebuke us for betraying our humanity, and they impel us to seek forgiveness in Christ.

Apply ————————————————————————————

■ Several times this passage speaks of the "day of God's wrath." How would you advise someone to prepare for that day?

This passage also speaks of the value of a healthy conscience. What influences have helped to shape your conscience?

What can you do now to point your conscience in a healthy direction?

God (who is perfect) shows no favoritism in his judgments. What are some ways that you can practice fairness in your own actions?

Pray————————————————————————————
■ Thank God that he is just and fair—showing no favoritism. Identify yourself in his presence as either Jew or Gentile. Thank him that through Jesus Christ he invites you into his family—regardless of your origins.

4
MISPLACED CONFIDENCE

Romans 2:17—3:8

W e place our confidence in all sorts of things for which we have no real proof. On a trip we trust that the road map shows exactly where the roads are, though we may close our eyes to the copyright date of five years ago. A wife trusts that her husband is calling from the office when he says that he is working late. We assume when a person hangs out a sign that says "doctor" that she really did graduate from medical school. Yet in each of these situations it is possible to misplace our confidence—with devastating results. If someone knows our error, it would be a kindness to point it out to us. Paul did so for the Jews in Rome.

Open ————————————————————————

■ What are some false assumptions that people make about gaining God's favor?

Study ————————————————————————

■ *Read Romans 2:17-29.* The argument of verses 17-24 is the same in principle as that of verses 1-3 and is just as applicable to us as to first-century critical moralizers and self-confident Jews. If we judge others, we should be able to judge ourselves (vv. 1-3). If we teach others, we should be able to teach ourselves (vv. 21-24). If we set ourselves up as either teachers or judges of others, we can have no excuse if we do not teach or judge ourselves. We cannot possibly plead ignorance. On the contrary, we invite God's condemnation of our hypocrisy.

---

1. The people described in verses 17-29 assumed that they had a good relationship with God. What kinds of things did they depend on to give them that relationship?

---

2. What is Paul trying to show his readers with the list of questions in verses 21-23?

---

3. In verse 24 Paul says, "God's name is blasphemed among the Gentiles because of you." Why?

---

4. What is the relationship between circumcision and keeping the law (vv. 25-29)?

5. What does it mean to have a circumcised heart (v. 29)?

6. How have you sensed the Spirit at work in your heart?

Summary: In this redefinition of what it means to be a Jew, an authentic member of God's covenant people, Paul draws a fourfold contrast. First, the essence of being a true Jew (who may indeed be ethnically a Gentile) is not something outward and visible, but inward and invisible. For the true circumcision is, second, in the heart, not the flesh. Third, it is effected by the Spirit, not the law, and fourth, it wins the approval of God rather than human beings. Human beings are comfortable with what is outward, visible, material and superficial. What matters to God is a deep, inward, secret work of the Holy Spirit in our hearts.

7. *Read Romans 3:1-8.* In what ways had the Jews "been entrusted with the very words of God"?

8. Notice the list of questions woven throughout verses 1-8. What objections to faith do these questions raise?

"It is often easier to follow Paul's arguments," writes C. K. Barrett, "if the reader imagines the apostle face to face with a heckler, who makes interjections and receives replies which sometimes are withering and brusque" (*A Commentary on the Epistle to the Romans* [Adam and Charles Black, 1962], p. 43). We may go further than this and picture Paul the Pharisee and Paul the Christian in debate with each other, as in Philippians 3.

9. How would you respond to a person who said, "I'm glad I fell so deeply into wrong. It shows how good God is and how much he will forgive" (vv. 5-8)?

10. This section of Romans ends with the words "Their condemnation is deserved." What did Paul mean?

Summary: We note from this passage (3:1-8) that Paul was not content only to proclaim and expound the gospel. He also argued its truth and reasonableness and defended it against misunderstanding and misrepresentation. Whether these Jewish objections were genuine (because he had actually heard them advanced) or imaginary (because he had made them up), he took them seriously and responded to them. He saw that the character of God was at stake. So he reaffirmed God's covenant as having abiding value, God's faithfulness to his promises, God's justice as judge, and God's true glory which is promoted only by good, never by evil.

Apply

■ If you are reading this book you have in some way been *entrusted* with the words of God. How are you using that responsibility?

The Jews to whom Paul was writing had all sorts of misplaced confidence about their special relationship with God. What or whom have you been tempted to trust besides the grace of Jesus Christ alone?

Pray ————————————————————————————

■ In Romans 2:24 Paul issues a strong accusation to Jews who knew God's law but did not keep it. Spend a few moments in self-examination to answer this question: "What do people think of God because of me?" Then talk to God about your findings.

5
UNHOLY
TOGETHERNESS

Romans 3:9-20

Whe like to choose the company we keep—and usually those choices are based on similarities. We go to church with people who share the same brand of Christian faith. We network with people of similar vocations. We join support groups of people who share a similar pain. We have coffee with people who live in the same neighborhood. We invite friendship with people who share a whole list of intangibles similar to our own. In doing so, we must admit that we are closing out people who are less like us in important ways. In the opening chapters of Romans Paul brings us up short about any haughty exclusivity in the company that we keep. He speaks of a togetherness that includes everyone—but it is an unholy togetherness.

Open
■ What kinds of "togetherness" have you chosen? Why?

Study

■ *Read Romans 3:9-18.* The apostle is approaching the end of his lengthy argument and asks himself how to wrap it all up, how to rest his case: "What shall we conclude then?" (v. 9).

He has exposed in succession the blatant unrighteousness of much of the ancient Gentile world (1:18-32), the hypocritical righteousness of moralizers (2:1-16) and the confident self-righteousness of Jewish people, whose anomaly is that they boast of God's law but break it (2:17—3:8). So now he arraigns and condemns the whole human race.

---

1. Paul opens this section of his letter with the words "What shall we conclude then?" In view of verses 9-12, what is his conclusion about all that he has said thus far?

---

2. Focus on verses 13-18. What images do these words bring to your mind?

---

3. Notice the various parts of the body that Paul describes. What impact does this have on the way you think about sin?

---

4. Verse 18 speaks of "fear of God." What kind of fear of God is appropriate?

5. How do you feel about seeing yourself described in the words of this passage?

Summary: One feature of this grim biblical picture stands out. It declares the *ungodliness* of sin. Sin is the revolt of the self against God, the dethronement of God with a view to the enthronement of oneself. Ultimately sin is self-deification, the reckless determination to occupy the throne which belongs to God alone.

---

6. *Read Romans 3:19-20.* According to these verses, what is an appropriate response to the law?

---

7. Suppose someone said, "Since no one will be 'declared righteous' by obeying God's law, why bother to pay any attention to it at all?" How would you respond?

I think Luther got it right when he said:

The principal point . . . of the law . . . is to make men not better but worse; that is to say, it sheweth unto them their sin, that by the knowledge thereof they may be humbled, terrified, bruised and broken, and by this means be driven to seek grace, and so come to that blessed Seed [sc. Christ]. (Commentary on St. Paul's Epistle to the Galatians [1531; James Clarke, 1953], p. 316.)

8. Paul opened his letter to the Romans with three and a half chapters on the topic of sin. What has this contributed to your view of yourself and your view of God?

9. How might these chapters affect your relationship to other people?

Summary: In conclusion, how should we respond to Paul's devastating exposure of universal sin and guilt? We should not try to evade it by changing the subject and talking instead of the need for self-esteem, or by blaming our behavior on our genes, nurturing, education or society. It is an essential part of our dignity as human beings that however much we may have been affected by negative influences, we are not their helpless victims, but rather responsible for our conduct. Our first response to Paul's indictment, then, should be to make it as certain as we possibly can that we have ourselves accepted this divine diagnosis of our human condition as true, and that we have fled from the just judgment of God on our sins to the only refuge there is, namely Jesus Christ, who died for our sins. For we have no merit to plead and no excuse to make. We too stand before God speechless and condemned. Only then shall we be ready to hear the great "But now" of verse 21, as Paul begins to explain how God has intervened through Christ and his cross for our salvation.

Apply

■ Many people today do not like to use words like *right, wrong* and *sin.* They value personal freedom and believe that they should do whatever seems appropriate in a particular setting. In view of the first three chapters of Romans, how do you respond to this kind of thinking?

Some people feel constantly guilty, plagued by false guilt. Others seem guilt-free, as if they have an inadequate sense of their own wrongdoing. But many people have a realistic view of personal sin. How would you describe your own sense of guilt and sin?

What hope would you offer someone who felt a constant nagging sense of guilt?

Pray————————————————————————————————
■ Prayerfully reread verses 10-18, acknowledging in the presence of God that this is a true description of yourself apart from the redeeming grace of Jesus Christ. Thank him for that grace.

6
FORGIVE US OUR DEBTS

Romans 3:21—4:25

*D*ebts are heavy burdens. Students graduate from college with debts higher than the cost of their parents' homes. Homes put their owners in debt for most of their working lives. Nations owe each other enough money to end poverty on both sides of their borders. But even debts this staggering can be paid off with hard work and cold cash. Resolving our debt to God is harder—maybe even impossible. Paul has spent three and a half chapters *proving* that we are all morally ruined, that we have no hope, regardless of our efforts, of earning God's favor.

Open

■ Bring to mind the largest financial debt you have ever had. Suppose you got a note from your creditor saying, "Someone else has paid your bill in full. You now owe nothing at all." What would you say and do?

Study

■ *Read Romans 3:21-31.* All human beings, of every race and rank, of every creed and culture, Jews and Gentiles, the immoral and the moralizing, the religious and the irreligious, are without any exception sinful, guilty, inexcusable and speechless before God. That was the terrible human predicament described in Romans 1:18—3:20. There was no ray of light, no flicker of hope, no prospect of rescue.

1. Paul opens this new section of Romans with the words "But now." What shift in emphasis do these words signal?

2. Verses 21-26 are six tightly packed verses, which Leon Morris suggests may be "possibly the most important single paragraph ever written" (p. 173). There is a host of theological terms. Give the best definition you can for each of these: righteousness, justified, grace, redemption, atonement, justice, faith. (A Bible dictionary or theological dictionary may help.)

3. Verse 22 says, "There is no difference." Find as many ways as you can in verses 21-31 that illustrate "no difference" between people.

4. Verse 27 says that we have no reason to boast. Why?

5. Verse 24 says that we "are justified freely by his grace." What day-to-day impact does this have on you?

Summary: Fundamental to the gospel of salvation is the truth that the saving initiative from beginning to end belongs to God the Father. No formulation of the gospel is biblical that removes the initiative from God and attributes it either to us or even to Christ. It is certain that we did not take the initiative, for we were sinful, guilty and condemned, helpless and hopeless. The first move was God the Father's, and our justification is "freely by his grace," his absolutely free and utterly undeserved favor. Grace is God loving, God stooping, God coming to the rescue, God giving himself generously in and through Jesus Christ

6. *Read Romans 4.* What words and phrases in this chapter seem important to you? Why?

7. Was Abraham justified by works or by faith? Explain your answer using information throughout chapter 4.

8. Romans 4:10 asks when Abraham was credited as righteous: after he was circumcised or before he was circumcised? What is the answer to that question, and what difference does it make (vv. 9-12)?

9. In what sense is Abraham "father of us all" (4:16)?

Jewish people were extremely conscious of their special covenant relationship with God, in which Gentiles did not share. It was to the Jews that God had entrusted his special revelation (3:2). Theirs too, as Paul will soon write, are "the adoption as sons . . . the divine glory, the covenants, the receiving of the law, the temple worship and the promises," not to mention "the patriarchs" and "the human ancestry of Christ" (9:4). What the Jews forgot, however, was that their privileges were not intended for the exclusion of the Gentiles, but for their ultimate inclusion when through Abraham's posterity "all peoples on earth" would be blessed.

10. Reread 4:7-8, which comes from Psalm 32:1-2. What is your own sense of blessing as you read those words?

11. God gives "life to the dead and calls things that are not as though they were" (4:17). What examples do you see of this in 4:18-25?

Summary: Woody Allen epitomizes for many an inability to cope with the prospect of death. "It's not that I'm afraid to die," he quips; "I just don't want to be there when it happens" (Graham McCann, *Woody Allen, New Yorker* [Polity Press, 1990], pp. 43, 83). But nothingness and death are no problem to God. On the contrary, it is out of nothing that he created the universe, and out of death that he raised Jesus. The creation and the resurrection were and remain the two major manifestations of the power of God.

Apply
◼ Jesus is alive! (4:23-25). How does this affect who you are or what you want to become?

Pick a favorite sentence from somewhere in Romans 3 or 4. Meditate on it word by word. Why is the sentence significant to you?

Pray
◼ Create a prayer based on the sentence you chose. Write or speak it as your personal offering to God.

7
PEACE WITH GOD

Romans 5:1—6:23

*P*eace is hard to come by in our fast-paced world. We mostly grab at it in bits and snatches: five minutes of peace just before the children thunder in from school, that last half-hour at work after the phones are shut off and everyone else has left the office, one quiet morning watching the sun rise over the Grand Canyon. After the first four chapters of Romans, with its overwhelming picture of human sinfulness against the backdrop of God's holiness, the idea that we might have peace with God is powerful indeed. Yet that is precisely what God offers.

Open
■ Describe one of your favorite mental pictures of peace.

Study
1. *Read Romans 5:1-11.* Pick a phrase or sentence in this section that you particularly appreciate. Why are these words significant to you?

We pause after Paul's first three affirmations about the "blessedness" of the justified, and reflect. The fruits of justification relate to the past, present and future. "We have peace with God" (as a result of our past forgiveness). "We are standing in grace" (our present privilege). "We rejoice in the hope of glory" (our future inheritance). Peace, grace, joy, hope and glory. It sounds idyllic. It is—except for Paul's fourth affirmation: *We also rejoice in our sufferings.*

---

2. Verse 2 says that we can rejoice even in our suffering. Why?

---

3. Verses 3-5 describe a sequence that begins with suffering and ends with hope—with several stages in between. When have you seen that sequence in yourself or in someone else?

---

4. Describe the work of Christ as seen in verses 6-11.

---

5. Paul uses the word *reconciliation* in verse 11. In view of his letter thus far, what does he mean by this term?

Summary: How can we doubt the love of God? To be sure, we are often profoundly perplexed by the tragedies and calamities of life. Indeed, Paul has been giving his teaching about God's love within the context of "tribulation," which can be very painful. But then we remember that God has both proved his love for us in the death of his Son (v. 8) and poured his love into us by the gift of his Spirit (v. 5). This is one of the most wholesome and satisfying features of the gospel. Objectively in history and subjectively in experience, God has given us good grounds for believing in his love.

---

6. *Read Romans 5:12-21.* Verses 12-17 speak of Adam and of Jesus Christ. What impact did each have on the human race? (Find all that you can.)

---

7. Notice the repeated pattern of "just as . . . , so also . . . " What comparisons does this phrase highlight?

The concept of our having sinned in Adam is certainly foreign to the mindset of Western individualism. We like to identify with Pilate, who washed his hands and declared his innocence. We were not guilty, we say; it had nothing to do with us. The apostles disagree. Not only did Herod and Pilate, Gentiles and Jews "conspire" against Jesus (Acts 4:27), but the sins which led to his death are our sins too. Moreover, if we turn away from God, we "are crucifying the Son of God all over again" (Hebrews 6:6). "Were you there," the Negro spiritual asks, "when they crucified my Lord?" The only possible answer is that we *were* there, and not merely as spectators, but as guilty participants. Horatius Bonar, the nineteenth-century Scottish hymn writer, expressed it well:

> 'Twas I that shed the sacred blood;
> I nailed him to the tree:
> I crucified the Christ of God;
> I joined the mockery.

---

8. *Read Romans 6.* In what various ways are the words *dead* and *alive* used in verses 1-14?

In what ways are these both a part of normal Christian experience?

9. Verse 5 says that Christians have been united to Christ in both his death and his resurrection. Why is this important (vv. 5-7)?

10. Verses 15-23 speak of slavery and freedom. What different forms of slavery and freedom do you see described here?

Summary: Romans 6 shows two lives which are totally opposed to each other. Jesus portrayed them as the broad road which leads to destruction and the narrow road which leads to life (Matthew 7:13). Paul calls them two slaveries. By birth we are in Adam the slaves of sin; by grace and faith we are in Christ the slaves of God. Bondage to sin yields no return except shame and ongoing moral deterioration, culminating in the death we deserve. Bondage to God, however, yields the precious fruit of progressive holiness, culminating in the free gift of life.

11. Focus on verse 23. How would you explain it to a ten-year-old child?

On May 28, 1972, the Duke of Windsor, the uncrowned King Edward VIII, died in Paris. The same evening a television program rehearsed the main events of his life. Extracts from earlier films were shown in which he answered questions about his upbringing, brief reign and abdication.

Recalling his boyhood as Prince of Wales, he said, "My father [King George V] was a strict disciplinarian. Sometimes when I had done something wrong, he would admonish me, saying, 'My dear boy, you must always remember who you are.'" It is my conviction that our heavenly Father says the same to us every day: "My dear child, you must always remember who you are."

Apply

■ In Romans 6:13 Paul invites us to use various parts of our bodies as "instruments of righteousness." What specific steps could you take in offering your body or any part of it to God?

Bring to mind a current area of suffering. How might the words of Romans 6:8-10 influence the way you deal with that suffering?

Pray

■ Romans 5 opens with the statement that "we have peace with God." Spend some time in silence before God. No need to say or do anything. Don't even try to pray during that silence. Just focus on God and the peace that he offers to you through Jesus Christ. Allow his peace to settle into your pores. After that period of silence, pray aloud, expressing your response to God.

8
BATTLING SIN

Romans 7:1-25

*R*omans 7 is known by many Christian people because of the debate it has provoked about holiness. Who is the "wretched man" of verse 24 who gives us such a graphic account of inner turmoil, cries out for deliverance and then immediately appears to thank God for it? Is this person a Christian or not yet a Christian? If a Christian, is he or she normal or abnormal, mature, immature, or fallen away? But it is never wise to bring to a passage of Scripture our own ready-made agenda, insisting that it answer our questions and address our concerns. For that is to dictate to Scripture instead of listening to it. If we come to Romans 7 with a mood of meekness and receptivity, it becomes evident at once that Paul's preoccupation is more historical than personal.

Open
■ When you hear the term "the law of God," what are some of your reactions?

Study

■ *Read Romans 7:1-6.* Paul is struggling with the place of the law in God's purpose. For the "law" or the "commandment" or the "written code" is mentioned in every one of the chapter's first fourteen verses and some thirty-five times in the whole passage, which runs from Romans 7:1 to 8:4. What is the place of the law in Christian discipleship now that Christ has come and inaugurated the new era?

---

1. What legal changes happen to a woman when her husband dies (vv. 1-3)?

---

2. What similar changes happen when we die to the law (vv. 4-6)?

---

3. Does this mean that Christians do not keep a moral code? (Use this passage as a basis for your answer.)

Summary: We can summarize three possible attitudes to the law, the first two of which Paul rejects, and the third of which he commends. We might call them "legalism," "antinomianism" and "law-fulfilling freedom." Legalists fear the law and are in bondage to it. Antinomians hate the law and repudiate it. Law-abiding free people love the law and fulfill it. Directly or indirectly Paul alludes to these three types in Romans 7.

---

4. *Read Romans 7:7-25.* Focus on verses 7-13. What is good about the law? Find all that you can.

---

5. What limitations do you see in these same verses to what the law can accomplish?

---

6. What influence has God's law had on you?

Take a criminal today. A man is caught red-handed breaking the law. He is arrested, brought to trial, found guilty and sentenced to prison. He cannot blame the law for his imprisonment. True, it is the law which convicted and sentenced him. But he has no one to blame but himself and his own criminal behavior. In a similar way Paul exonerates the law. It is indwelling sin which, because of its perversity, is aroused and provoked by the law. Those who say that our whole problem is the law are quite wrong. Our real problem is not the law, but sin. It is indwelling sin which accounts for the weakness of the law, as the apostle will go on to show in the next paragraph. The law cannot save us because we cannot keep it, and we cannot keep it because of indwelling sin.

7. Focus on verses 14-25. What makes this person a "wretched man"?

8. What examples of this kind of struggle have you seen in your own life?

9. Paul says in verse 18, "I have the desire to do what is good, but I cannot carry it out." What does this imply about a person's relationship with God?

10. In spite of this conflict, why is Paul thankful (vv. 24-25)?

Summary: We return to the question whether the law is still binding on Christians and whether we are expected still to obey it. Yes and no! Yes in the sense that Christian freedom is freedom to serve, not freedom to sin. We are still slaves (v. 6), slaves of God and of righteousness (6:18, 22). But also no, because the motives and means of our service have completely changed. Why do we serve? Not because the law is our master and we have to, but because Christ is our husband and we want to. Not because obedience leads to salvation, but because salvation leads to obedience. And how do we serve? "We serve in the new way of the Spirit" (v. 6). For the indwelling of the Holy Spirit is the distinguishing characteristic of the new age, and so of the new life in Christ.

Apply

■ Paul addresses three approaches to God's law: legalism (you have to obey it), antinomianism (you just ignore it) and law-fulfilling freedom (you don't count on keeping the law to make you right with God, but you love God's law and enjoy following it). Which best describes your own current relationship with God's law? If this is different from some other stage of your life, what caused the change?

Verse 24 says, "What a wretched man I am! Who will rescue me from this body of death?" Using your knowledge of Scripture as well as your own experience with God, how would you answer that person?

Pray

■ Use Romans 7:4-6 as the focus of your prayer. Praise God for the way he is revealed there, thank him for what he offers, confess your sins as these words reveal them to you and ask God to continue his work in your life.

9
RESCUED BY GOD'S SPIRIT

Romans 8:1-17

*I*t's been a long uphill climb through the first seven chapters of Romans. Paul has convinced us of our sin, of God's holiness and of our inability to meet the demands of God's law. He has even shown us a picture of the bitter inner battle when we try to get ourselves into spiritual shape under our own steam. It's true, as we have climbed this mountain, that Paul has allowed us glimpses of God's grace. He showed us God's faithfulness to Abraham (who was far from perfect), he offers peace and joy through Christ (even in the midst of suffering), and he offers us hope, aliveness, because Jesus Christ is alive, raised from the dead. But in the first half of Romans, after these brief breaks of light, Paul keeps us firmly trudging the path of discovering our own helplessness apart from the mercy of God.

But in Romans 8 everything changes. It's as if we have finally reached the summit and an enormous vista full of the wonders of God's gifts to his people opens before us. We should approach it with appropriate thanksgiving and awe.

Open

■ When and how have you seen God's kindness?

Study

■ *Read Romans 8:1-8.* Romans 8 is without doubt one of the best-known, best-loved chapters of the Bible. If in Romans 7 Paul has been preoccupied with the place of the law, in Romans 8 his preoccupation is with the work of the Spirit. In chapter 7 the law and its synonyms were mentioned some thirty-one times, but the Holy Spirit only once (v. 6), whereas in the first twenty-seven verses of chapter 8 he is referred to nineteen times by name. The essential contrast which Paul paints is between the weakness of the law and the power of the Spirit. For over against indwelling sin, which is the reason the law is unable to help us in our moral struggle (7:17, 20), Paul now sets the indwelling Spirit.

1. According to verses 1-4, what all has God done?

2. In what different ways might people respond to these actions by God?

3. How have you responded at various stages of your life?

4. In spite of having written seven chapters about sin and our inability to keep God's law, Paul now writes, "Therefore, there is now no condemnation." Why?

5. Focus on verses 5-8. How is a mind "set on what nature desires" different from a mind "set on what the Spirit desires"?

Summary: Here are two categories of people (the unregenerate who are "in the flesh" and the regenerate who are "in the Spirit") who have two perspectives or mindsets ("the mind of the flesh" and "the mind of the Spirit"), which lead to two patterns of conduct (living according to the flesh or the Spirit) and result in two spiritual states (death or life, enmity or peace). Thus our mind, where we set it and how we occupy it, plays a key role in both our present conduct and our final destiny.

---

6. *Read Romans 8:9-17.* Drawing on the information in verses 9-11, what do you learn about the Holy Spirit?

---

7. What do the same verses reveal about the Trinity?

The ultimate destiny of our body is not death, but resurrection. Paul points out this truth in verse 11. Our bodies are not yet redeemed (v. 23), but they will be, and we are eagerly awaiting this event. How can we be so sure about it? Because of the nature of the indwelling Spirit. He is not only "the Spirit of life" (v. 2), but also the Spirit of resurrection.

---

8. Focus on verses 12-17. What do you enjoy in these verse? Why?

---

9. What further work of the Holy Spirit do you see in these verses?

10. What affect does it have on you that you can speak to God as "Father"?

Summary: F. F. Bruce reminds us that we must interpret the implications of our adoption in terms not of our contemporary culture but of the Greco-Roman culture of Paul's day. He writes: "The term 'adoption' may have a somewhat artificial sound in our ears; but in the Roman world of the first century A.D. an adopted son was a son deliberately chosen by his adoptive father to perpetuate his name and inherit his estate; he was no whit inferior in status to a son born in the ordinary course of nature, and might well enjoy the father's affection more fully and reproduce the father's character more worthily" (*The Letter of Paul to the Romans*, 2nd ed. [Leicester: Inter-Varsity Press, 1985], p. 157).

Apply
■ What are some ways that you can show your appreciation for being adopted into God's family?

The Christian life is essentially life in the Spirit, a life which is animated, sustained, directed and enriched by the Holy Spirit. Without the Holy Spirit true Christian discipleship would be inconceivable, and indeed impossible. In view of all that this passage reveals about the Holy Spirit, how can you give appropriate attention to his presence in your life?

Pray
■ Focus on the work of the Spirit in you, praying for a growing awareness of the Holy Spirit's work.

10
PRESENT PAIN, FUTURE GLORY

Romans 8:18-39

*L*ife is hard. Sure, it has its moments of joy: birth, weddings, the seashore. But joy is often shrouded in pain. Birth gets linked with death, weddings with divorce, and the sea with pollution. It is an imperfect world, and we are all imperfect people.

But there is good news. Romans 8 tells us that it won't always be that way! There is a future glory. God will change his people; he is in the process of changing us right now. Even the earth will be a part of that glory. But for now we wait—and ever so slowly move toward what we will become.

Open ───────────────────────────────

■ Theologians sometimes say that we live in the "already, but not yet." Christians are *already* a part of God's family, but they are *not yet* living in the perfect world God designed, *nor* are they *yet* perfect physically, mentally or spiritually themselves. What do you long for that is a part of your "not yet"?

Study

■ *Read Romans 8:18-27.* Paul now moves on from the present ministry of God's Spirit to the future glory of God's children, of which indeed the Holy Spirit is "the firstfruits" (v. 23). What prompted this development was clearly his allusion to our sharing in the sufferings and glory of Christ (v. 17). For "suffering and glory" is the theme throughout this section, first the sufferings and glory of God's creation (vv. 19-22) and then the suffering and glory of God's children (vv. 23-27).

---

1. What examples of present suffering do you see in verses 18-27?

---

2. How is the "future glory" described?

---

3. Verses 24-25 speak of hope. What is the hope that is defined here?

In what practical ways can you express this sort of hope?

---

4. Notice the three uses of the word *groan* in this passage. This word is like the groaning of childbirth; it anticipates the birth of something new. What does each use of this word suggest about suffering and about hope?

5. Focus on verses 26-27. What do you appreciate about the Holy Spirit's work as it is described here?

Summary: Why do we not know what to pray for? Perhaps because we are unsure whether to pray for deliverance from our sufferings or for strength to endure them. Also, since we do not know what we will be, or when or how, we are in no position to make precise requests. So the Spirit intercedes for us and does so with speechless groans. It is truly amazing that having written of the groaning creation and of the groaning church, Paul should now write of the groaning Spirit. God's creation and God's children groan because of their present state of imperfection, but there is nothing imperfect about the Holy Spirit. It must be, therefore, that the Holy Spirit identifies with our groans, with the pain of the world and the church, and shares in the longing for the final freedom of both. We and he groan together.

6. *Read Romans 8:28-39.* Focus on verses 28-30. What five actions does God take toward his people? (Define each as accurately as you can.)

7. In view of these actions of God, what encouragement do you find in verse 28?

Paul has already several times used the noun *glory*. It is essentially the glory of God, the manifestation of his splendor, of which all sinners fall short (3:23) but which we rejoice in hope of recovering (5:2). Paul also promises both that if we share Christ's sufferings we will share his glory (8:17) and that the creation itself will one day be brought into the freedom and glory of God's children (8:21). Now he uses the verb: "Those he justified, he also glorified." Our destiny is to be given new bodies in a new world, both of which will be transfigured with the glory of God.

---

8. Find five questions in verses 31-39. What is the cumulative impact of these questions?

---

9. What do these verses reveal about God?

---

10. How might the love of God, as it is revealed here, help you deal with some of your current pain?

Summary: Here then are five convictions about God's providence (v. 28), five affirmations about his purpose (vv. 29-30) and five questions about his love (vv. 31-19), which together bring us fifteen assurances about him. We urgently need them today, since nothing seems stable in our world any longer. Insecurity is written across all human experience. Christian people are not guaranteed immunity to temptation, tribulation or tragedy, but we are promised victory over them. God's pledge is not that suffering will never afflict us, but that it will never separate us from his love. Our confidence is not in our love for him, which is frail, fickle and faltering, but in his love for us, which is steadfast, faithful and persevering. The doctrine of "the perseverance of the saints" needs to be renamed. It is the doctrine of the perseverance of God with the saints.

Apply

■ What signs of a "groaning" creation are particularly painful to you?

What signs do you see of your own incompleteness—compared to our future glory?

How is God's love nudging you toward that future glory?

Pray

■ Reread verses 26-27. Invite the participation of the Holy Spirit as you approach God in prayer. Ask him to show you how to pray, who to pray for, how to express your praise and thanks, what gifts to ask from God. Then approach Father God in the name of his Son, Jesus Christ. As Romans 8 points out, prayer is a *Trinitarian* exercise.

11
UNDERSTANDING GOD'S PURPOSES

Romans 9

Certain questions are perennial in college dorms and seminary classrooms. These questions often deal with the purpose of life, the nature of God, and what difference it all makes anyway. One of the more jarring questions for Christians revolves around what happens to those outside the Christian faith. "No one comes to the Father except through me," said Jesus Christ in the fourteenth chapter of John. Those words are warm and comforting to the Christian believer—until they encounter a dear friend who happens to be a non-Christian. Then an onslaught of similar questions explodes: What about those who have never heard about Jesus? What about good people who happen to believe in some other religion? Are all of these people eternally lost? What about the unbelieving Jews Paul addressed?

Paul treats these questions with respect. Indeed, he had once been one of those Jews devoted to the ancient faith of the Hebrews.

Open

■ Suppose a friend says to you, "I think your Christianity is much too exclusive. People travel on all kinds of spiritual journeys, and I think that

God accepts them all." How would you respond?

Study ——————————————————————————

■ *Read Romans 9:1-18.* Is it wrong to question God? Paul is not addressing someone who asks sincerely perplexed questions, but rather someone who "quarrels" with God, who talks back or answers back. Such a person manifests a spirit of rebellion against God a refusal to let God be God and acknowledge his or her true status as creature and sinner. Instead of such presumption we need, like Moses, to keep our distance, take off our shoes in recognition of the holy ground on which we stand, and even hide our face from him (Exodus 3:5). Similarly, we need, like Job, to put our hand over our mouth, confess that we tend to speak things we do not understand, despise ourselves, and repent in dust and ashes (Job 40:4; 42:3, 6).

---

1. What phrases here show the intensity of Paul's concern for the Jewish people (vv. 1-3)?

---

2. What privileges had God already granted the Jews (vv. 4-5)?

---

3. Four questions outline this chapter. (See verses 6 [a statement], 14, 19, and 30.) How would you phrase each question?

---

4. When and why have you asked a question similar to one of these?

5. Focus on verses 6-13. Does being a descendant of Abraham guarantee a spot in God's family? Why or why not?

---

6. How do the examples of Moses, Pharaoh and a potter help answer the question about God's justice?

Verse 13 says, "Jacob I loved, but Esau I hated." This bald statement sounds shocking in Christian ears and cannot possibly be taken literally. Although there is such an emotion as "holy hatred," it is directed only to evildoers and would be inappropriate here. God put Jacob above Esau—as individuals, not just in the sense that Israelites were God's people, not the Edomites. We have to remember that Esau forfeited his birthright because of his own worldliness (Genesis 25:29-34) and lost his rightful blessing because of his brother's deceit (Genesis 27), so human responsibility was interwoven with divine sovereignty in their story. We should also recall that the rejected brother was circumcised and therefore in some sense too a member of God's covenant and promised lesser blessings. Nevertheless Esau illustrates the key truth of "God's purpose according to election." So God's promise did not fail.

Read Romans 9:22-33. Few preachers maintained balance better than Charles Simeon of Cambridge in the first half of the nineteenth century. He ministered at a time when there was much controversy surrounding the doctrine of election. In defense of his commitment to both election and individual freedom, Simeon would sometimes borrow an illustration from the Industrial Revolution: "As wheels in a complicated machine may move in opposite directions and yet subserve a common end, so may truths apparently opposite be perfectly reconcilable with each other, and equally subserve the purposes of God in the accomplishment of man's salvation" (Preface to the *Horae Homileticae* in 21 volumes [1832], p. 5).

---

7. What examples do you see of God's wrath and his mercy in verses 22-24?

---

8. How had the prophets Hosea and Isaiah prepared the Jewish people for the possibility that belonging in God's family was not simply a matter of biological heritage (vv. 25-29)?

---

9. Focus on verses 30-33. What relationships do you see here between faith, works, Jews and Gentiles?

---

10. What do you learn about Jesus Christ from verse 33?

---

11. How have you seen Christ in one of the ways described here?

Summary: Paul began this chapter with the paradox of Israel's privilege and prejudice (vv. 1-4). How can her unbelief be explained?

It is not because God is unfaithful to his promises, for he has kept his word in relation to the Israel within Israel (vv. 6-13).

It is not because God is unjust in his "purpose according to election," for neither his having mercy on some nor his hardening of others is incompatible with his justice (vv. 14-18).

It is not because God is unfair to blame Israel or hold human beings accountable, for we should not answer him back, and in any case he has acted according to his own character and according to Old Testament prophecy (vv. 19-29).

It is rather because Israel is proud, pursuing righteousness in the wrong way, by works instead of faith, and so has stumbled over the stumbling block of the cross (vv. 30-33).

Thus this chapter about Israel's unbelief begins with God's purpose of election (vv. 6-29) and concludes by attributing Israel's fall to her own pride (vv. 30-33).

Apply ———————————————————————————
■ This chapter speaks several times of God's mercy. When and how have you seen God's mercy at work?

Paul speaks of people who did not come into God's family because instead of trusting in the "rock" they stumbled over it (vv. 32-34). Who among your friends and family seem to have made that same mistake?

Mentally select one of these people who do not yet believe. Try to see Christianity from that person's point of view. How do you think he or she sees the Christian faith?

Pray ————————————————————————————
■ Spend time praying for people you know who have not yet trusted Christ. Ask God to extend his mercy to them and draw them into faith. Ask him to show you how you might become a part of that mercy.

12
GOD'S GRIEF

Romans 10

*F*or two thousand years God had courted his people. Sometimes they walked with him as did Abraham, the first of the Hebrews. Some performed marvelous acts of faith as did Nehemiah, rebuilding the walls of Jerusalem, as did Jeremiah, wailing over the sins of his people as he called them back to God. Many were flawed, serving God in one event and defying him in another. Jonah, for example, nearly drowned before agreeing to perform his assignment and preach to Nineveh. Even then he complained that God forgave such sinful people as the Ninevites. Samson did more for the cause of God in his suicidal death than in his unruly life. And some among God's people were evil to the core. The evil king Manasseh, who ruled longer than any other king, took delight in killing the prophets. King Ahab stole a poor man's vineyard, and, when the prophet Elijah confronted him, Ahab spent the rest of his life trying to destroy him.

Behind the headlines of individual Hebrew heroes and villains, however, were generations of others. Sometimes they served God, often they rebelled, sometimes they repented. But always they were *his* people. Until now. God the Father had provided one eternal way to belong to him: his Son, Jesus Christ. What if his chosen people rejected his Son? The closing verses of this chapter record poignant words from God, "All day long I have held out my hands to a disobedient and obstinate people."

Open ————————————————————————

■ When have you seen the sadness of a ruptured relationship?

Study ————————————————————————

■ *Read Romans 10:1-13.* One of the notable features of Romans 10 is that it is saturated with Old Testament allusions and quotations. Paul cites Scripture here in order to confirm or illustrate eight truths: first, the ready accessibility of Christ to faith (vv. 6-8 = Deuteronomy 30:12); second, the promise of salvation to all who believe (v. 11 = Isaiah 28:16; v. 13 = Joel 2:32); third, the glorious necessity of evangelism (v. 15 = Isaiah 52:7); fourth, the unresponsiveness of Israel (v. 16 = Isaiah 53:1); fifth, the universality of the gospel (v. 18 = Psalm 19:4); sixth, the Gentiles' provocation of Israel (v. 19 = Deuteronomy 32:21); seventh, the divine initiative of grace (v. 20 = Isaiah 65:1); and eighth, the patient grief of God the evangelist (v. 21 = Isaiah 65:2). Thus Paul's emphasis is not only on the authority of Scripture, but also on the fundamental continuity which unites the Old and the New Testament revelations.

1. Focus on verses 1-4. Describe Paul's attitude toward the Jews.

2. What were the strengths and what were the inadequacies of their religion?

3. Paul quotes the teachings of Moses about the law—but he applies those teachings to Jesus (vv. 5-8). What is appealing about "the righteousness that is by faith"?

---

4. Verses 9-13 contain an ancient creed of the Christian faith. According to these verses, what defines a Christian?

---

5. What words and phrases in verses 11-13 express the invitation offered by God?

---

6. How might the message of Romans 10 affect your relationships with other Christians?

with those who have not yet come to saving faith?

Summary: What then, according to this section, is necessary for salvation? First the fact of the historic Jesus Christ, incarnate, crucified, risen, reigning as Lord and accessible. Second, the apostolic gospel, "the word of faith" (v. 8), which makes him known. Third, simple trust on the part of the hearers, calling on the name of the Lord, combining faith in the heart and confession with the mouth. But still something is missing. There is, fourth, the evangelist who proclaims Christ and urges people to put their trust in him. It is of Christian evangelists that Paul writes in the next paragraph.

7. *Read Romans 10:14-21.* Notice the four questions of verses 14-15 and the explanation in verses 16-19. According to these verses, what are the usual steps toward becoming a Christian?

8. Paul quotes Isaiah in verse 15. What is the significance of the quotation in this context?

The essence of Paul's argument is seen if we put his six verbs in opposite order: Christ sends heralds, heralds preach, people hear, hearers believe, believers call, and those who call are saved. And the relentless logic of Paul's case for evangelism is felt most forcibly when the stages are stated negatively and each is seen to be essential to the next.

9. In verses 19-21 Paul again quotes Moses and Isaiah. What do these verses show about God's actions toward people—and their response to him?

10. What do these verses reveal about God's relationship with the Jews?

Summary: God deliberately reverses the roles between himself and the Gentiles. It would normally be for them to ask, seek and knock (as Jesus was later to put it), and to adopt toward him the respectful attitude of a servant at his master's disposal, saying, "Here I am." Instead, although they did not ask or seek or offer themselves to his service, he allowed himself to be found by them, he revealed himself to them, and he even offered himself to them, saying humbly to them, "Here am I." This is dramatic imagery for grace, God taking the initiative to make himself known: "All day long I have held out my hands to an obstinate people" (Isaiah 65:2).

These Jews did not even give him the neutral response of the Gentiles, who decline both to ask and to seek. No, their response is negative, resistant, dismissive. They are determined to remain "an obstinate people." We feel God's dismay, his grief.

Apply

■ Verse 9 says that Christians confess, "Jesus is Lord." Make a mental review of what you have said and done in the last week. In what ways have you confessed that Jesus is your Lord?

Verses 14-18 speak of the importance of sharing the good news of Jesus with those who do not yet believe. What can you do to take part in that task?

Pray

■ If God can grieve over Jewish unbelievers, so can we. Bring to mind a Jewish acquaintance, or if you do not have any acquaintances who are Jewish, bring to mind a Jewish person mentioned or pictured in the media. Intercede for this person in prayer. Ask that God will continue to extend his hand, that in time he or she will confess that Jesus is Lord.

13
A DEEP-ROOTED TREE

Romans 11

*B*ristlecone pine grows at certain high elevations in the American southwest. This strange and sturdy tree survives on the dry, windy rims of canyons. Amazingly, bristlecone pine lives for centuries—1600 years or more, adapting to harsh conditions with an appearance best described as the "tortured tree look." While the main trunk can appear dead for decades, pointing barren bony fingers toward the sky, some other section, even a single branch, grows crisp, short needles and prickly cones, granting continued survival. They make a strange combination, this whitened skeleton yoked at the root to startling green life. Paul drew a similar picture of God's people.

Open
■ What are some of your personal "roots" in the Christian faith?

Study
■ *Read Romans 11:1-24.* How could God cause people not to believe in himself? Verse 7 says, "The others," the unbelieving Israelite majority, "were

hardened." There can be little doubt that Paul meant they were hardened by God (since the next verse says, "God gave them a spirit of stupor"). Nevertheless, as with the hardening of Pharaoh and those he represented (9:18; 11:25), a judicial process is in mind ("a retribution," in fact, v. 9) by which God gives people up to their own stubbornness. What this "hardening" means in practice Paul goes on to indicate from two Old Testament quotations, both of which refer to eyes which cannot see.

1. Verses 1 and 11 voice two questions as an outline to this section of Paul's letter. In view of what Paul has said so far, why are these reasonable questions?

2. Focus on verses 1-10. How might the experience of Elijah be a comfort to Jewish converts to Christianity (vv. 2-5)?

3. How would you describe the tension between grace and works (vv. 5-6)?

4. What do you find troubling in verses 7-10?

5. Focus on verses 11-24. What does the tree with the grafted branch express about the relationships between God, the Jews and the Gentiles?

6. Verse 22 says, "Consider therefore the kindness and sternness of God." Which of these qualities are you likely to emphasize over the other? What dangers could this unbalanced emphasis create?

In 1905 Sir William Ramsay wrote an interesting article about the process of grafting Paul describes. Paul's reference, he said, is not to "the ordinary process of grafting the young olive-tree" but to "the method of invigorating a decadent olive-tree" (W. Robertson Nicoll, ed., *The Expositor,* 6th series, vol. XI [Hodder and Stoughton, 1905], pp. 24, 34). In this case what is "contrary to nature" is not the "grafting" but the "belonging," namely that the shoot has been cut from the wild olive tò which it naturally belonged and has been grafted into the cultivated olive to which it does not naturally belong (John Ziesler, *Paul's Letter to the Romans* [SCM, 1989], p. 281). Paul develops his allegory in such a way as to play on the themes of "broken off" and "grafted in" and to teach two complementary lessons. The first is a warning to the Gentile believers not to presume (vv. 17-22), and the second a promise to the Israelite unbelievers that they could be restored (vv. 23-24).

Read Romans 11:25-36. The three main words in verse 26, namely *all, Israel* and *saved,* need some investigation. First, what is the identity of "Israel" which is to be saved? The natural interpretation of the "mystery" is that Israel as a people is hardened until the fullness of the Gentiles has come in, and then at that point (it is implied) Israel's hardening will be over and "all Israel will be saved."

Second, there is the word *all.* Whom does Paul intend to include in "all Israel"? At present Israel is hardened except for a believing remnant and will remain so until the Gentiles have come in. Then "all Israel" must mean the great mass of the Jewish people, comprising both the previously hardened majority and the believing minority. It need not mean literally every single Israelite. This is in keeping with contemporary usage.

The third word is *saved.* According to verses 26-27, the deliverer would come to bring his people to repentance and so to forgiveness, according to God's covenant promise. It is clear from this that the "salvation" of Israel for which Paul has prayed (10:1), to which he will lead his own people by arousing their envy (11:14), which has also come to the Gentiles (11:11; 1:16), and which one day "all Israel" will experience (11:26) is salvation from sin through faith in Christ.

---

7. Focus on verses 25-32. What reasons for hope do you find here?

---

8. The mercy of God comes up several times in these verses. In what ways are both Jews and Gentiles recipients of God's mercy?

---

9. How have you seen God's mercy at work?

---

10. Study the doxology of verses 33-36. How is God's character reflected in this song of praise?

---

11. Chapters 9—11 of Romans, often called "the Jewish section," have a long reputation for difficult interpretation. How is this doxology a fitting close to this part of Paul's letter?

Summary: Disobedience is likened to a dungeon in which God has incarcerated all human beings so that "they have no possibility of escape except as God's mercy releases them" (Charles E. B. Cranfield, *A Critical and Exegetical Commentary on the Epistle to the Romans*, vol. II [T&T Clark, 1979], p. 587). This human disobedience is the prison from which divine mercy liberates us. Paul has been at pains to argue that there is no distinction between Jews and Gentiles, either in sin (3:9, 22) or in salvation (10:12). Now he writes that as they have been together in the prison of their disobedience, so they will be together in the freedom of God's mercy.

Apply

■ Verse 20 advises readers, "Do not be arrogant, but be afraid." What are some ways that you can express appropriate humility about your relationship with God?

Verses 11-21 draw a powerful image of an olive tree with a cut-off branch and a wild branch grafted in, drawing life from its deep roots. What strengths can you draw from this root system of the ancient Hebrew faith? how?

Pray

■ Spend time meditating phrase by phrase on the doxology of verses 33-36. Next, use each phrase as a starting point for your prayers of praise.

14
GETTING PRACTICAL

Romans 12:1-8

*P*aul used the first eight chapters of his letter to the Romans to explain more completely than in any other book of the Bible the whole sweep of the Christian faith. He opens with our sin and therefore our need for a Redeemer. He speaks of faith, righteousness and judgment. He offers justification through faith and peace with God through Jesus Christ. He outlines the continued struggle with sin, then rises to one of the peak passages of Scripture as he illustrates in Romans 8 a picture of life through God's Spirit and our future glory with him. Paul then takes three chapters to deal with the pressing question of God's relationship with the Jews—in view of Gentile converts to Christianity. Once again we see God's justice, but we also see justice tempered by his mercy and persistent love.

Now in Romans 12 Paul stands on the sturdy theology of the previous eleven chapters and says, "Let's get practical." And *practical* is the theme of the last five chapters of his letter. Here we learn how to get along with other Christians, the importance of love, why we should not seek revenge, what to do about a hostile government, how to approach someone whose rules are not to our liking, and ways to wait for Christ's return. In the end we even see Paul's personal notes to friends—reflecting a broad, comfortable range of companionship in faith. But even in this final section of his book, Paul does not abandon theology. He just shows us how to live it out.

Open
■ Do you consider yourself more practical or theoretical in your approach to faith? Explain.

Study

■ *Read Romans 12:1-2.* One of the notable features of Paul's teaching is that he regularly combines doctrine with duty, belief with behavior. In consequence, as in some of his other letters, he now turns in Romans 12 from the gospel to everyday Christian discipleship. Moreover, it is not only individual or personal ethics to which Paul now introduces his readers. He is concerned to depict the characteristic of the new community which Jesus has brought into being by his death and resurrection.

1. Using the content of verses 1-2, describe in your own words an appropriate response to God's mercy.

2. Notice that these verses speak of both mind and body. Why are both of these important in our relationship with God?

3. What are some practical ways that you could offer your body as a living sacrifice to God?

4. What are some steps you have taken (or could take) toward the renewing of your mind?

Summary: What is this living sacrifice, this rational, spiritual worship? It is not to be offered in temple courts or in the church building, but rather in home life and in the marketplace. It is the presentation of our bodies to God. This blunt reference to our bodies was calculated to shock some of Paul's Greek readers. Brought up on Platonic thought, they will have regarded the body as an embarrassing encumbrance. Their slogan was "the body is a tomb," in which the human spirit was imprisoned and from which it longed for its escape. Still today some Christians feel self-conscious about their bodies. The traditional evangelical invitation is what we give our hearts to God, not our bodies. But no worship is pleasing to God that is purely inward, abstract and mystical; it must express itself in concrete acts of service performed by our bodies.

---

5. *Read Romans 12:3-8.* Study verse 3. What information here would help you to accurately evaluate yourself?

---

6. Twice this verse uses the word *think.* How can the mind contribute to either a healthy or an unhealthy view of ourselves?

The link between Paul's general appeal (vv. 1-2) and his particular instructions which now follow (vv. 3-8) seems to be the place of the mind in Christian discipleship. Our renewed mind, which is capable of discerning and approving God's will, must also be active in evaluating ourselves, our identity and our gifts. For we need to know who we are and to have an accurate, balanced and above all sober self-image. A renewed mind is a humble mind, like Christ's (Philippians 2:5-11).

7. In what ways is a group of Christians like a single body? (Compare the word *body* in verses 1, 4 and 5.)

8. Study the list of gifts in verses 6-8. What can you know about their source, purpose and variety?

9. How might each contribute to the well-being of other Christians?

Summary: This list of seven spiritual gifts in Romans 12 is much less well-known than either the two overlapping lists in 1 Corinthians 12 (nine in the first list and eight in the second) or the short list of five in Ephesians 4:11. The 1 Corinthians list focuses on the supernatural (tongues, prophecy, healing and miracles), whereas in Romans 12 all the gifts apart from prophecy are either general and practical (service, teaching, encouragement and leadership) or even prosaic (giving money and doing acts of mercy). It is evident that we need to broaden our understanding of spiritual gifts.

Apply ——————————————————————————

■ God has given each of his people special skills to be used for the good of other Christians. Think of yourself with some of the "sober judgment" described in verse 3. Without falling into either pride or self-deprecation, what are some of the skills or gifts that God has given you?

How might knowing that these gifts come from God keep you from either arrogance or belittling yourself?

Name several specific ways that you can use one or more of your skills to serve other Christians.

Pray ————————————————————————

■ Ask God to show you your gifts. Name the gifts you are aware of, giving thanks even for the most simple and obvious. Take time to use your "renewed mind" to think and consider how God wants you to put these gifts to use. Ask God to show you ways to offer them as a "living sacrifice" for his glory and for the strengthening of his people.

As an expression of your body as a "living sacrifice" (12:1), you might cup your hands as you pray, showing that you have received these gifts from God. Then raise your hands toward heaven to symbolize that you are willingly offering that gift back to him in his service.

15
SHOWING LOVE

Romans 12:9-21

*L*ove is hard. Yet the Christian faith is founded on love—the love of God for his people and the love of his people for each other. Jesus himself said, "By this all men will know that you are my disciples, if you love one another" (John 13:35). So it should be no surprise that Paul bases the practical section of his letter on expression of love. We can be grateful that he nowhere says that we must love others by feeling warm toward them. While God graces our lives with a few who bring out warm feelings in us, many people who need love are not exactly lovable. Paul does us the favor of stressing not the feelings of love, but the actions.

Open ——————————————————

■ What would people in your church or fellowship group say about how easy or difficult it is to show you love?

Study ——————————————————

■ *Read Romans 12:9-16.* Without doubt *agapē* love now dominates the scene. So far in Romans all references to *agapē* have been to the love of God—demonstrated on the cross (5:8), poured into our hearts (5:5) and doggedly refusing to let us go (8:35, 39). But now Paul focuses on *agapē* as the essence of Christian discipleship. Romans 12—15 are a sustained exhortation to let love govern and shape all our relationships.

---

1. What expressions of love do you find in verses 9-16? (Find all that you can.)

---

2. Many of the statements of how to express love also include a negative—what *not* to do. What can you learn from each negative?

---

3. When has receiving one of the expressions of love described here made a major impact on you?

---

4. Thoughtfully consider your church or fellowship group. Which of these expressions of love do you regularly see there? (*Who* does *what* to show that love?)

---

5. Which of these expressions of love need to be more apparent in your church or fellowship group?

Summary: What a comprehensive picture of Christian love Paul gives us! Love is sincere, discerning, affectionate and respectful. It is both enthusiastic and patient, both generous and hospitable, both benevolent and sympathetic. It is marked by both harmony and humility. Christian churches would be happier communities if we all loved one another like that.

---

6. *Read Romans 12:17-21.* Several times in verses 17-21 Paul uses the words "Do not . . ." What general themes do you see in what we are *not* to do?

---

7. Paul follows each use of the phrase "do not" with what we are to do instead. In view of these instructions how are we to deal with people who might otherwise be our enemies?

What does it mean to "heap burning coals on his head"? Because in the Old Testament it is said that God will "rain fiery coals" on the wicked (Psalm 11:6; 140:10), some take the coals here as a symbol of judgment and even argue that to serve our enemies "will have the effect of increasing the punishment" which they will receive (Robert Haldane, *Exposition of the Epistle to the Romans,* vol. 2 [1835-39; Sovereign Grace Book Club, 1957], p. 574). But the whole context cries out against this explanation, especially the very next verse and its reference to overcoming evil with good. Others suggest that the pain inflicted by the burning coals is a symbol of the shame and remorse experienced by an enemy who is rebuked by kindness. A third option is that the coals are a symbol of penitence. Recent commentators draw attention to an ancient Egyptian ritual in which a penitent would carry burning coals on his head as evidence of the reality of his repentance.

---

8. It is easy, almost natural, to be "overcome by evil" (v. 21). We simply join what is going on around us. How might following the principles in this passage lead us instead to overcome evil?

9. Focus on verse 18. How might the note of realism expressed here encourage you about difficult relationships in your life?

10. In what practical ways might this passage from Romans 12 help you to obey Christ's command to "Love your enemies, do good to those who hate you" (Luke 6:27)?

Summary: In all our thinking and living it is important to keep the negative and positive counterparts together. Both are good. It is good never to retaliate, because if we repay evil for evil, we double it, adding a second evil to the first and so increasing the tally of evil in the world. It is even better to be positive, to bless, to do good, to seek peace, and to serve and convert our enemy, because if we thus repay good for evil, we reduce the tally of evil in the world while at the same time increasing the tally of good. To repay evil for evil is to be overcome by it; to repay good for evil is to overcome evil with good. This is the way of the cross.

Apply ——————————————————————

■ Few of us have people we would label as enemies. But most of us have difficult people in our lives, people whose interests and values are so different from our own that we could hardly think of them as friends. Bring to mind one of these people who has particularly made your life difficult. Skim through Romans 12:9-21 with this person in mind. What do you find here that might lead you to "live at peace"?

What practical step could you take in that direction?

Consider your relationships within your church, fellowship group or family. In view of verses 9-16, what is one way that you could better express your love to one person?

Pray ─────────────────────────────

■ Verse 12 says that we are to be "faithful in prayer." Ask God to show you how you might show your love for God and your love for other people through your praying.

16
CONSCIENTIOUS CITIZENSHIP

Romans 13

*A*re politics dirty? It seems so—on testimony of the evening TV news and the morning newspaper headlines. Political corruption is so common that we merely sigh at the latest revelation of sexual misconduct or financial scandal. What is a responsible Christian to do in this environment? We hardly know whether to run for office or refuse to vote.

Those decisions were not a lot easier in Paul's era. Paul lived in a country occupied by Roman intruders. We must remember that these same intruders accepted a trumped-up charge and executed by capital punishment the Lord Jesus Christ. Surely his zealous apostle would advocate the overthrow of such a hostile government. Not so. Instead Paul's principles for living within the government are remarkably similar for living within the church.

Open

■ What was the attitude toward government in the home where you grew up?

Study

1. *Read Romans 13:1-7.* Verse 1 says that we are to submit to governing authorities. Why? (Find all that you can in vv. 1-7.)

2. Verses 6-7 say that we are to pay our debts. According to these verses what all might we owe the government?

3. How might the principles of verses 1-7 influence what you say and do during the heat of an election campaign?

4. Relations between church and state have been notoriously controversial throughout the Christian centuries. To oversimplify, four main models have been tried—Erastianism (the state controls the church), theocracy (the church controls the state), Constantinanism (the compromise in which the state favors the church and the church accommodates to the state in order to retain its favor), and partnership (church and state recognize and encourage each other's distinct God-given responsibilities in a spirit of constructive collaboration). Which is most like what Paul is teaching here and why?

5. No government is perfect, and some governments are cruel and corrupt. If you were under a cruel and corrupt government, how could you follow the underlying principles of Romans 13 and still do what is right?

Summary: We need to be cautious in our interpretation of Paul's statements. He cannot be taken to mean that all the Caligulas, Herods, Neros and Domitians of New Testament times, and all the Hitlers, Stalins, Amins and Hussains of our times, were personally appointed by God, that God is responsible for their behavior, or that their authority is in no circumstances to be resisted. Paul means rather that all human authority is derived from God's authority, so that we can say to rulers what Jesus said to Pilate, "You would have no power over me if it were not given to you from above" (John 19:11). Pilate misused his authority to condemn Jesus; nevertheless, the authority he used to do this had been delegated to him by God.

---

6. *Read Romans 13:8-14.* We sometimes think of law as being harsh and unyielding, while we see love as soft and flexible. Yet Paul speaks of both law and love in the same paragraph (vv. 8-10). What connections do you see between love and the commandments?

---

7. How might the laws listed here show us practical ways to express love? (Think of tempting situations where these laws would give you guidance toward love.)

---

8. No love is perfect, not even love for ourselves. Even so, how can the admonition "Love your neighbor as yourself" (v. 9) lead us toward a godly expression of love?

---

9. According to verses 11-14, how are we to prepare ourselves for Christ's return?

10. What does verse 11 mean by "our salvation is nearer now than when we first believed"?

---

11. What are some ways that you can "clothe yourselves with the Lord Jesus Christ" (v. 14)?

Summary: Romans 13 began with important teaching about *how* we can be good citizens (vv. 1-7) and good neighbors (vv. 8-10); it ends with *why* we should be. There is no greater incentive for doing these duties than a lively expectation of the Lord's return. We will be rightly related to the state (which is God's minister) and to the law (which is fulfilled in loving our neighbor) only when we are rightly related to the day of Christ's coming. Although both the state and the law are divine institutions, they are provisional structures, which one day will cease. That day is steadily approaching. Our calling is to live in the light of it, to behave in the continuing night as if the day had dawned, to enjoy the "now already" of the inaugurated kingdom in the certain knowledge that what is still "not yet," namely the consummated kingdom, will soon arrive.

Apply ———————————————————————————

■ Verse 12 says that "the day [of Christ's return] is almost here." Of course, we cannot know whether that event will take place in another two thousand years or quite soon indeed. In view of that uncertainty, what kind of person do you want to be when you meet Jesus—whenever that happens?

Focus on the command "Love your neighbor as yourself." Consider ways that you express understanding and care for yourself. Next bring to mind a person to whom you ought to be more loving. How might you extend some of those same kindnesses to that person?

Pray————————————————————————————————
■ The early section of Romans 13 deals with conscientious citizenship. Pray today for one person who holds government responsibility.

17
LIVING BY SOMEONE ELSE'S RULES

Romans 14

*I*t must have been hard in the early church. One small, new church—perhaps meeting in a home—contained Jews who wouldn't touch any food that wasn't kosher, Gentiles who relished all food, slaves who might be more spiritually mature than their masters—who might also be Christian. Even the worship date must have been a struggle. Jews believed God's holy day was from sundown Friday until sundown Saturday. Gentiles had begun to observe Sunday for worship—because Christ rose from the dead on Sunday, so they called Sunday the "Lord's Day." And how were they to observe religious holidays? Special feast days for the Roman gods and goddesses hardly seemed appropriate, especially to converts out of paganism. But neither did a lot of the Jewish holy days—at least not to Gentile Christians.

How were these first-century Christians to worship together, eat together, even marry each other? Somehow they had to determine what was important, what was not, and how to treat each other when they disagreed about unimportant issues.

Open ——————————————————

■ What "nonessentials" have you seen Christians quibble about? With what results?

Study

■ *Read Romans 14:1-12.* Both previous chapters of Romans have laid emphasis on the primacy of love, whether loving our enemies (12:9, 14, 17-21) or loving our neighbors (13:8-10). Now Paul supplies a lengthy example of what it means to "walk according to love." It concerns the relations between two groups in the Christian community in Rome whom he names "the weak" and "the strong": "We who are strong ought to bear with the failings of the weak" (15:1).

It is important to be clear at the outset that Paul is referring to a weakness neither of will nor of character, but of "faith" (14:1). So if we are trying to picture a weaker brother or sister, we must not envisage a vulnerable Christian easily overcome by temptation, but a sensitive Christian full of indecision and scruples. What the weak lack is not strength of self-control but liberty of conscience.

---

1. What "disputable matters" had the potential of dividing the Christians at Rome (vv. 1-8)?

---

2. What principles here would help us worship together with Christians who disagree on matters that are not essential to the faith?

---

3. How would you explain that it is right for one Christian to abstain from meat out of service to the Lord while another Christian can eat the same meat and give thanks to God (vv. 6-8)?

---

4. If you could say with another believer, "Whether we live or die, we belong to the Lord," how would this assurance affect the way you would handle disagreements with that person? (Consider information in verses 7-11.)

---

5. Paul says in verse 7, "None of us lives to himself alone," yet in verse 12 he says, "Each of us will give an account of himself to God." In what practical ways can you live out both this unity and this individuality in your church or fellowship group?

Summary: We must not elevate nonessentials, especially issues of custom and ceremony, to the level of essential and make them tests of orthodoxy and conditions of fellowship. Nor must we marginalize fundamental theological or moral questions as if they were only cultural and of no great importance. Paul distinguished between these things; so should we.

But what are *nonessentials?* The sixteenth-century Reformers called such things "matters of indifference." In our day we might mention such practices as the mode of baptism, Episcopal confirmation (whether it is a legitimate part of Christian initiation), and the use of cosmetics, jewelry and alcohol. We differ regarding such beliefs as which gifts of the Spirit are available and/or important, whether miraculous "signs and wonders" are intended to be frequent or infrequent, how Old Testament prophecy has been or will be fulfilled, when and how the millennium will be established, the relation of history to eschatology, and the precise nature of both heaven and hell. In these and other issues, today as in first-century Rome, the problem is how to handle conscientious differences in matters on which Scripture is either silent or seemingly equivocal, in such a way as to prevent them from disrupting Christian fellowship.

6. *Read Romans 14:13-23.* Why might a Christian follow someone else's rules—even though those rules are more strict than his or her own? (Draw from throughout verses 13-23.)

---

7. What, according to this passage, are some of the harmful things that can happen if a person who is strong in faith refuses to give in on these nonessential matters of conscience?

---

8. What harm have you seen come from Christian disagreements over minor issues?

The disputable matters of which Paul speaks are ceremonial or cultural (not moral) issues, for Paul is quite explicit that some of our thoughts, words and deeds are intrinsically evil. The apostle's argument now is that whenever the strong insist on using their liberty to eat whatever they like, even at the expense of the welfare of the weak, they are guilty of a grave lack of proportion. They are overestimating the importance of diet (which is trivial) and underestimating the importance of the kingdom (which is central). Paul has used a little irony to expose the incongruity of valuing food above peace and the health of our stomach above the health of the community.

9. Study verse 17. What do you see here that might help you through a disagreement with another Christian?

---

10. Verses 22-23 speak of both freedom and faith. How do you enjoy both of these in your Christian experience?

Summary: The outline of Paul's argument in this long section (14:1— 15:13) seems to be as follows. First he lays down the fundamental principle of acceptance (especially acceptance of the weak) which undergirds the whole discussion. It is positive ("Accept him"), yet qualified ("without passing judgment on disputable matters." Then, covering the rest of the passage, he develops three negative deductions which follow from his positive principle. He tells his readers that they must neither despise nor condemn the weak (vv. 1-13); that they must neither offend nor destroy them (13-23); and that they must not please themselves but follow Christ's unselfish example (15:1-4). In conclusion he celebrates the union of Jews and Gentiles in the worship of God (15:5-13).

Apply ————————————————————————

■ What are some of your own "disputable matters," nonessential subjects where some of your Christian friends are more strict than you are?

In discussing and acting on those matters, how can you reflect the teachings of Romans 14?

Are you being too restrictive yourself in some areas—forcing other Christians to adjust to your limitations? How could you begin to grant your friends freedom and respect in matters that are not central to the Christian faith—and still obey your own conscience?

Pray

■ Pray for an enlightened heart. It takes much study of Scripture and great discernment of our own prejudices and preferences to accurately define what is a core *essential* of the Christian faith and what is simply (rightly or wrongly) our own interpretation of Scripture and our preferred practice. Bring some of these matters to God in prayer. Ask him to show you what you ought to hold on to as core truth—and what you ought to leave to personal preference. Then ask God to search your heart with the goal of correcting any lack of tolerance you may have for other Christians who disagree with you on the unimportant matters.

18
UNITY, LIBERTY & CHARITY

Romans 15:1-13

*U*nity, liberty, charity. These are the building blocks of healthy relationships whether in a church, family or cluster of friends. Unity says that we choose to stay together. Liberty says that we respect each other as individuals and allow certain freedoms because of that respect. Charity says that we give love even when it is not deserved—and that we allow ourselves to receive love even when we do not deserve it. But even in healthy organizations, these three important forces pull against each other. Group unity infringes on personal liberty. Charity is humbling to receive—and inconvenient to give. So how can we achieve these powerful goals in our Christian relationships—and hold them in appropriate balance?

Open

■ Describe the presence of unity, liberty and charity among Christians in your church or fellowship group.

Study

1. *Read Romans 15:1-7.* Romans 15:1 begins, "We who are strong . . ." What responsibilities do Christians strong in faith have toward weaker Christians (vv. 1-7)?

2. This passage says that we are to please our neighbors, not ourselves. Why (vv. 3-4)?

3. According to verse 4, what are some of the characteristics of Scripture?

4. Paul offers a prayer for the Roman Christians in verses 5-6 and then instructions in verse 7. What, according to these verses, is a healthy church to look like?

5. What connections do you see between healthy human relationships and worship?

6. Verses 5-7 use the phrases "endurance," "encouragement," "spirit of unity," "one heart and mouth, "glorify God" and "accept one another." When have you experienced one or more of these with other believers?

Summary: With verse 7 Paul returns to the beginning, to his original and positive appeal for acceptance. Indeed, the long, closely reasoned, theological-practical argument about the strong and the weak (14:2—15:6) is sandwiched between the two cries "Accept him" (14:1) and "Accept one another" (v. 7). Both are addressed to the whole congregation, although the first urges the church to welcome the weaker brother, while the second urges all church members to welcome each other. Both also have a theological base. The weaker one is to be accepted "for God has accepted him" (14:3), and the members are to welcome each other "just as Christ accepted you" (v. 7). Moreover, Christ's acceptance of us was also "in order to bring praise to God" (v. 7). The entire credit for the welcome we have received goes to him who took the initiative through Christ to reconcile us to himself and to each other.

---

7. *Read Romans 15:8-13.* How many times does Paul mention the term *Gentiles* in verses 8-11? What is the point of this repetition?

---

8. How do these four quotes from the Old Testament help Jewish and Gentile Christians work and worship together?

With verse 8 Paul slips almost imperceptibly from the unity of the weak and the strong through Christ to the unity of Jews and Gentiles through the same Christ. Although the Old Testament contains many prophecies of the inclusion of the Gentiles, and indeed the promise to Abraham was that the nations would be blessed through his posterity, yet God had made no covenant with the Gentiles comparable to his covenant with Israel. Consequently, it was in mercy to the Gentiles, as it was in faithfulness to Israel, that Christ became a servant for the benefit of both.

9. Focus on Paul's prayer of blessing in verse 13. In what ways is this prayer an outgrowth of all that he has taught about weak and strong Christians?

10. What in this prayer do you desire for yourself?

Summary: One area in which the distinction between faith and love should operate is in the difference between essentials and nonessentials in Christian doctrine and practice. Although it is not always easy to distinguish between them, a safe guide is that truths on which Scripture speaks with a clear voice are essentials, whereas whenever equally biblical Christians, equally anxious to understand and obey Scripture, reach difference conclusions, these must be regarded as nonessentials.

In fundamentals, faith is primary, and we may not appeal to love as an excuse to deny essential faith. In nonfundamentals, however, love is primary, and we may not appeal to zeal for the faith as an excuse for failures in love. Faith instructs our own conscience; love respects the conscience of others. Faith give liberty; love limits its exercise. No one has put it better than Rupert Meldenius.

In essentials unity;
In nonessentials liberty;
In all things charity.

Apply

■ With whom do you most need to put to work the principles of unity, liberty and charity described above? What steps can you take in that direction?

How can (or does) your own worship reflect the unity and diversity of other Christians?

Pray

■ It is a spiritual pleasure to create prayer from the words of Scripture. Paul gives two prayers in this section of his letter: a prayer for the group of Roman Christians (vv. 5-6) and a prayer for individuals (v. 13). Pray God's words back to him by using these biblical prayers to intercede for groups and individuals who need the blessings asked here. Just read the words of Scripture aloud to God, inserting names where appropriate.

19
SHARING
THE MISSION

Romans 15:14-33

Nearing the conclusion of his letter, Paul wonders if he has offended his readers by the fact, contents or tone of his letter. Has he been presumptuous to address a church he did not found and has never visited? Has he given the impression that he regards their Christianity as defective and immature? Has he been too outspoken? The apostle seems to be experiencing a twinge of apprehension about how his letter will be received.

In the rest of the letter Paul writes very personally. He opens his heart to them about the past, present and future of his ministry, he asks humbly for their prayers, and he sends many greetings. In these ways he gives us insight into the outworking of God's providence in his life and work.

Open

■ When have you enjoyed being a small part of something much bigger than you could accomplish alone?

Study

1. *Read Romans 15:14-22.* According to verses 14-16, why did Paul write to the Romans?

2. Describe the assignment God had given to Paul (vv. 15-16).

3. What are some of the features of Paul's work thus far (vv. 17-21)?

4. What kinds of power were evident in Paul's ministry?

5. What do you see in Paul's ministry that you would like to imitate in your own work for God? (Consider Paul's attitude as well as his accomplishments.)

Summary: Paul concludes: "This is why I have often been hindered from coming to you" (v. 22). In the first chapter Paul wrote that he had "many times" planned to visit them, but had so far "been prevented" (1:13), although he did not divulge what had stopped him. Now he does. It had to do with his mission policy. On the one hand, because he was concentrating on pioneer evangelism elsewhere, he was not free to come to them. On the other hand, because the Roman church had not been founded by him, he did not feel at liberty to come and stay. Soon, however, as he is about to explain, he will visit them, since he will only be "passing through" (v. 24) on his way to the unevangelized field of Spain.

6. *Read Romans 15:23-33.* Paul's letter to the Romans was probably written from the church in Corinth in about A.D. 57. What do these verses reveal about Paul's travel plans? (Look for places and distance.)

7. Why was Paul headed for Jerusalem (vv. 26-29)?

___

8. The significance of Paul's journey to Jerusalem (the solidarity of God's people in Christ) was primarily neither geographical (from Greece to Judah), nor social (from rich to the poor), nor even ethnic (from Gentiles to Jews), but both religious (from liberated radicals to traditional conservatives, that is, from the strong to the weak) and especially theological (from beneficiaries to benefactors). What principles regarding the relationship between Christians—even those separated by distance and ideology—does Paul's effort suggest?

Summary: Clearly Paul saw great significance in making this offering, as may be seen partly in the disproportionate amount of space which he devoted to it in his letters (see also 1 Corinthians 16:1-4 and specifically 2 Corinthians 8—9), partly from the passionate zeal with which he promoted it, and partly from his astonishing decision to add nearly 2,000 miles to his journey, in order to present the offering himself. Instead of sailing directly west from Corinth to Rome to Spain, he has made up his mind to travel first in entirely the wrong direction, that is, to go to Rome via Jerusalem. The so-called "gift" was in reality a "debt." The nature of this debt Paul has already elaborated in chapter 11.

___

9. What instructions for praying does Paul give to his Roman readers (vv. 30-33)?

___

10. What principles for praying can you gather from these brief instructions?

Some people tell us, in spite of Paul's earlier statement that "we do not know what we ought to pray for" (8:26), that we should always be precise, specific and confident in what we pray for, and that to add "if it be your will" is a cop-out and incompatible with faith. In response, we need to distinguish between the general and the particular will of God. Since God has revealed his general will for all his people in Scripture (that we should control ourselves and become like Christ), we should indeed pray with definiteness and assurance about these things. But God's particular will for each of us (for example, regarding a life work or a life partner) has not been revealed in Scripture, so in praying for guidance it is right to add "by God's will." If Jesus himself did this in the garden of Gethsamane ("Not my will, but yours be done," Luke 22:42), and if Paul did it twice in his letter to the Romans, we should do it too. It is not unbelief, but a proper humility.

Apply ───────────────────────────────────

■ Take stock of your habits of prayer. What are some ways that you can (or do) express appropriate humility in your praying?

───────────────────────────────────

According to verse 24, Paul assumes that when he arrives in Rome the Christians there will "assist me on my journey." (He probably meant housing while in Rome as well as provisions and possibly companionship for the next leg of the trip.) In what ways can you assist the work of Christ?

Summary: So what happened to Paul's three prayers, namely that he might be rescued from unbelievers in Jerusalem, that his gift might be accepted, and that he might succeed in reaching Rome? Were they answered or unanswered? Regarding the middle of the three prayers we do not know, since surprisingly Luke does not refer to the offering in his Acts narrative, although he knows about it, because he accompanied Paul to Jerusalem and records Paul's statement (when on trial before Felix) that he had come to Jerusalem "to bring my people gifts for the poor" (Acts 24:17). The probability is that the gifts were accepted.

What, then, about the other two petitions? Was Paul delivered from unbelievers in Jerusalem? No, in the sense that he was arrested, tried and imprisoned, but also yes because he was three times rescued from lynching (Acts 21:30-32; 22:22-24; 23:10), once from flogging (Acts 22:25-29) and once from a plot to kill him (Acts 23:12-35). Then did he reach Rome? Yes indeed, as Jesus had promised him he would (Acts 23:11), but neither when nor how he had expected, for he arrived about three years later as a prisoner and after an almost fatal shipwreck.

So prayer is an essential Christian activity, and it is good to ask people to pray for us and with us, as Paul did. But there is nothing automatic about prayer. Prayer is not like using a coin-operated machine or a cash dispenser. The struggle involved in prayer lies in the process of coming to discern God's will and to desire it above everything else. Then God will work things out providentially according to his will, for which we have prayed.

Pray————————————————————————————
■ In verse 30 Paul asks the Roman Christians to "join me in my struggle by praying to God for me." He did not see prayer as a passive duty but as an active sharing in his ministry. Pray today for someone involved in the work of Christ. As you pray, picture that person's needs, emotions, spiritual struggles and ordinary tasks—as well as the larger picture of how his or her work fits into the broad parameters of God's kingdom. Through your ministry of prayer, participate in that work.

20
KEEPING FRIENDS

Romans 16

We all have different patterns of friendships. Some people want dozens and dozens of friends—but nothing too intense. Others prefer only two or three friends, but they will share their hearts with them. Some people create their best friendships around work or neighborhood where the ordinary events of life bring them in constant contact. Other friendships grow ut of pivotal life events like college or summer camp or the death of someone close to each. For some people their entire social life is the church; all of their friendships grow there. A few people seem to have almost no friends at all. They may even appear to like it that way. Whatever our style of making friends, maintaining these relationships takes certain talent. Friendship thrives on appreciation and mutuality. The closing notes of Paul's letter shows us a picture of his friends—and what he enjoyed about them.

Open ─────────────────────────────

■ Describe one of your long-standing friendships.

Study

1. *Read Romans 16:1-16.* Study the list of twenty-six people in verses 1-16. What does the list reveal about the way Paul conducted his relationships?

2. Notice the phrases Paul uses to describe his friends. What are some ways that he gives a sense of dignity to his friends even in a mere greeting?

3. What indications do you see of diversity among the people Paul felt close to? (If necessary, do a little research about names and backgrounds in this list.)

4. What concepts expressed in this list of greetings show an undergirding unity within that diversity?

5. What do you see in the relationships implied by Paul's greetings that you would like to incorporate in your own friendships?

One of the most interesting and instructive aspects of church diversity in Rome is that of gender. Nine out of the twenty-six persons greeted are women. Two names call for special attention. The first is Priscilla, who in verse 3 and in three other New Testament verses is named in front of her husband (Acts 18:18, 26; 2 Timothy 4:19). Whether the reason was spiritual (that she was converted before him or more active in Christian service than he) or social (that she was a woman of standing in the community) or temperamental (that she was the dominant personality), Paul appears to recognize and not to criticize her leadership.

The prominent place occupied by women shows that Paul was not at all the male chauvinist of popular fantasy. Does it also throw light on the vexed question of the ministry of women? As we have seen, among the women Paul greets, three were hard workers in the Lord's service. Priscilla was one of Paul's "fellow-workers," Junia was a well-known missionary, and Phoebe may have been a deaconess. On the other hand, it has to be said that none of them is called a presbyter in the church, even though an argument from silence can never be decisive.

---

6. *Read Romans 16:17-27.* What last-minute warnings did Paul write in verses 17-19?

---

7. In practical terms, what does it mean to be wise about what is good and innocent about what is evil? (How can we go about achieving that wisdom and innocence?)

Verse 20 holds a certain tension. Enjoying peace and crushing Satan do not sound altogether compatible with each other. But God's peace allows no appeasement of the devil. It is only through the destruction of evil that true peace can be attained. So far this victory has been fulfilled only in Christ, since God has put "all things under his feet" (Ephesians 1:22-23; Hebrews 2:8). Yet still his exaltation is incomplete, for while he reigns, he also waits for his enemies to be made his footstool (Psalm 110:1). That this will happen "soon" is not necessarily a time reference, but rather a

---

statement that God has planned nothing to occupy the space between the Ascension and the Second Coming. Meanwhile, the Romans should expect regular interim victories over Satan, partial crushing of him under their feet. Such victories would be impossible, however, apart from grace. So Paul adds: "The grace of our Lord Jesus be with you."

---

8. Not only does Paul send greetings to his friends in Rome; he also sends greetings from eight of the friends who are with him. What additional information do you gain here about Paul's circle of friends (vv. 21-23)?

---

9. Study Paul's closing prayer of praise in verses 25-27. What words and phrases here echo previous segments of Paul's letter?

---

10. Paul's prayer begins with the statement that God is able to "establish" us by the gospel. In what ways does the book of Romans establish your faith?

Summary: Paul concludes his book in praise of God's wisdom (v. 27). God's wisdom is seen in Christ himself, "in whom are hidden all the treasures of wisdom and knowledge" (Colossians 2:3), above all in his cross which, though foolish to human beings, is the wisdom of God (1 Corinthians 1:24), in God's decision to save the world not through its own wisdom but through the folly of the gospel (1 Corinthians 1:21), in the extraordinary phenomenon of the emerging multiracial, multicultural church (Ephesians 3:10), and in his purpose ultimately to unite everything under Christ (Ephesians

1:7-10). No wonder Paul has already broken out in praise of God's wisdom: "Oh, the depth of the riches of the wisdom and knowledge of God!" (11:33). No wonder he does it again at the end of his letter.

Apply
■ Bring to mind a dozen or so of your closest friends and coworkers. Follow Paul's example and give a brief summary of what you appreciate about each. (Try to find an opportunity to mention your appreciation to them in person.)

Paul closes his letter with a prayer of praise for God's wisdom and a desire for God's eternal glory. What are some ways that you have seen God's glory revealed in your friends?

in your own experience?

Pray
■ Create a prayer based on Paul's closing prayer of verses 15-27. Meditate on each phrase. Pray each phrase in your own words, adding personal notes. As you near the end of the prayer, consider God's wisdom and respond to him accordingly.

Guidelines for Leaders

My grace is sufficient for you. (2 Corinthians 12:9)

If leading a small group is something new for you, don't worry. These sessions are designed to be led easily. Because the Bible study questions flow from observation to interpretation to application, you may feel as if the studies lead themselves.

You don't need to be an expert on the Bible or a trained teacher to lead a small group discussion. As a leader, you can guide group members to discover for themselves what the Bible has to say and to listen for God's guidance. This method of learning will allow group members to remember much more of what is said than a lecture would.

This study guide is flexible. You can use it with a variety of groups—students, professionals, neighborhood or church groups. Each study takes forty-five to sixty minutes in a group setting.

There are some important facts to know about group dynamics and encouraging discussion. The suggestions listed below should equip you to effectively and enjoyably fulfill your role as leader.

Preparing for the Study

1. Ask God to help you understand and apply the passage in your own life. Unless this happens, you will not be prepared to lead others. Pray too for the various members of the group. Ask God to open your hearts to the message of his Word and motivate you to action.

2. Read the introduction to the entire guide to get an overview of the topics that will be explored.

3. As you begin each study, read and reread the assigned Bible passage to familiarize yourself with it.

4. This study guide is based on the New International Version of the Bible. It will help you and the group if you use this translation as the basis for your study and discussion.

5. Carefully work through each question in the study. Spend time in meditation and reflection as you consider how to respond.

6. Write your thoughts and responses in the space provided in the study guide. This will help you to express your understanding of the passage clearly.

7. You may want to get a copy of the Bible Speaks Today commentary by John Stott that supplements the Bible book you are studying. The commentary is divided into short units on each section of Scripture so you can easily read the appropriate material each week. This will help you answer tough questions about the passage and its context.

It may help to have a Bible dictionary handy. Use it to look up any unfamiliar words, names or places. (For additional help on how to study a passage, see *How to Lead a LifeGuide Bible Study* from InterVarsity Press, USA.)

8. Take the "Apply" portion of each study seriously. Consider how you need to apply the Scripture to your life. Remember that the group members will follow your lead in responding to the studies. They will not go any deeper than you do.

Leading the Study

1. Begin the study on time. Open with prayer, asking God to help the group to understand and apply the passage.

2. Be sure that everyone in your group has a study guide. Encourage the group to prepare beforehand for each discussion by reading the introduction to the guide and by working through the questions in each study.

3. At the beginning of your first time together, explain that these studies are meant to be discussions, not lectures. Encourage the members of the group to participate. However, do not put pressure on those who may be hesitant to speak during the first few sessions.

4. Have a group member read aloud the introduction at the beginning of the discussion.

5. Every session begins with an "open" question, which is meant to be asked before the passage is read. These questions are designed to introduce the theme of the study and encourage group members to begin to open up. Encourage as many members as possible to participate, and be ready to get the discussion going with your own response.

These opening questions can reveal where our thoughts or feelings need to be transformed by Scripture. That is why it is especially important not to read the passage before the question is asked. The passage will tend to color the honest reactions people would otherwise give because they are, of course, supposed to think the way the Bible does.

6. Have a group member read aloud the passage to be studied.

7. As you ask the study questions, keep in mind that they are designed to be used just as they are written. You may simply read them aloud. Or you may prefer to express them in your own words.

There may be times when it is appropriate to deviate from the study guide. For example, a question may have already been answered. If so, move on to the next question. Or someone may raise an important question not covered in the guide. Take time to discuss it, but try to keep the group from going off on tangents.

8. Avoid answering your own questions. If necessary repeat or rephrase them until they are clearly understood. Or point the group to the commentary woven into the guide to clarify the context or meaning without answering the question. An eager group quickly becomes passive and silent if members think the leader will do most of the talking.

9. Don't be afraid of silence in response to the discussion questions. People may need time to think about the question before formulating their answers.

10. Don't be content with just one answer. Ask, "What do the rest of you think?" or "Anything else?" until several people have given answers to the question.

11. Acknowledge all contributions. Try to be affirming whenever possible. Never reject an answer. If it is clearly off-base, ask, "Which verse led you to that conclusion?" or again, "What do the rest of you think?"

12. Don't expect every answer to be addressed to you, even though this will probably happen at first. As group members become more at ease, they will begin to truly interact with each other. This is one sign of healthy discussion.

13. Don't be afraid of controversy. It can be very stimulating. If you don't resolve an issue completely, don't be frustrated. Explain that the group will move on and God may enlighten all of you in later sessions.

14. Periodically summarize what the group has said about the passage. This helps to draw together the various ideas mentioned and gives continuity to the study. But don't preach.

15. Conclude your time together with conversational prayer, adapting the prayer suggestion at the end of the study to your group. Ask for God's help in following through on the commitments you've made.

16. End on time.

Many more suggestions and helps can be found in *How to Lead a LifeGuide Bible Study* and *The Big Book on Small Groups* (both from InterVarsity Press, USA) or *Housegroups* (Crossway Books, UK). Reading through one of these books would be worth your time.

For Further Reading
from InterVarsity Press

The Bible Speaks Today by John Stott
The books in this practical and readable series are companions to the John Stott
Bible Studies. They provide further background and insight into the passages.

The Message of Acts
The Message of Ephesians
The Message of Galatians
The Message of Romans (UK title), *Romans* (US title)
The Message of the Sermon on the Mount (Matthew 5—7)
The Message of 1 & 2 Thessalonians
The Message of 1 Timothy & Titus (UK title), *1 Timothy & Titus* (US title)
The Message of 2 Timothy